THE BUGGIES STILL RUN

Warren S. Kissinger

The Brethren Press
Elgin, Illinois

First Church of the Brethren
1340 Forge Road
Carlisle, Pennsylvania 17013

THE BUGGIES STILL RUN

Copyright © 1983, by The Brethren Press, Elgin, Ill.

Cover Design by Guy Wolek

Library of Congress Cataloging in Publication Data

Kissinger, Warren S., 1922-
    The buggies still run.

    1. Christian sects — Pennsylvania — Lancaster County. 2. Pennsylvania Dutch — Pennsylvania — Lancaster County. 3. Lancaster County (Pa.) — Description and travel. 4. Simplicity — Religious aspects — Christianity. 5. Peace (Theology) 6. Fellowship. 7. Tobacco — Pennsylvania — Lancaster County. 8. Akron (Pa.) 9. Kissinger, Warren S., 1922-   . I. Title.
BR555 .P5L363 1982   280'.4'0974815   82-12976
ISBN 0-87178-123-9

Published by The Brethren Press,
    Elgin, Illinois 60120

Printed in the United States of America

To

Jean
John
David
Ann
Adele

Companions on life's pilgrimage

Lancaster County

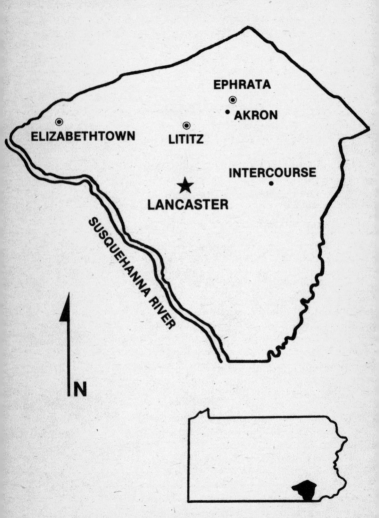

EPHRATA

AKRON

ELIZABETHTOWN

LITITZ

INTERCOURSE

★ LANCASTER

SUSQUEHANNA RIVER

N

Contents

Foreword

As Americans we are a problem to the rest of the world because we lack the historical experience and wisdom to match (and tame) the power and influence we exercise. True, we collect antiques, and gawk at the exotic subcultures that survive in our midst. Indeed, we spend excessive energy fighting the few traditions that do crop up. For the most part, however, downgrading the past is part of the American way.

In recent decades the mood has begun to change. Spurred in part by the rise of "Black consciousness," immigrant groups in the United States developed new interest in their particular heritage. In the early 1970s, this shift in mood was hailed as the "new ethnicity." Though the importance of the ethnic renaissance was likely exaggerated at the time, more than a passing fad was involved.

The "plain people" in "Pennsylvania Dutch" country have long exercised a certain charm precisely because they are people wedded to a tradition in a relatively traditionless society. Paradoxically, however, the growth of sympathy in the society for subcultural minorities has certain deleterious consequences for the plain people. I refer to the intrusions of the tourist trade on the communities themselves. Quite apart from that particular problem, the strains by pressures and inducements of the host society are becoming on the "plain people" communities themselves.

As Warren Kissinger demonstrates in this volume, the frontier zone between a major and minority culture is a zone rich in human experience. Kissinger, a native of the Pennsylvania Dutch country (Akron, Pennsylvania), and a Church of the Brethren minister, professor, writer, and editor, offers in these pages a delightful kaleidoscopic view of the "plain people" odyssey. Currently a classifier of religious books at the

Library of Congress in Washington, D. C., Kissinger will confront a tough challenge when *The Buggies Still Run* arrives on his desk for classification. This book contains studies in theology, in religious history, in social history, in autobiography—the list can be extended.

As a writer frequently in trouble with editors, I shall not presume to comment on the interweaving of themes and modes that run throughout the volume. But therein lies part of the charm and power of the volume, and how appropriately so! The interweaving of the "sacred" and the "profane," of "theology" and "life" is germane to the ways of the plain people. No idiom, then, could be more appropriate than the one Kissinger chooses.

Kissinger describes his approach as "sympathetically-critical." The "plain people" are the various groups of Brethren, Mennonites, and related bodies. Puzzling, of course, given their pacifist commitment, is the splintering so prevalent among them. The splintering arises, not for theological, but for practical reasons, practical having to do with cultural applications in religious communities seeking to embrace the whole of life. Through these complexities, Kissinger moves gently, sensitively, and respectfully. Theological training at Yale during a distinguished era there sharpens his natural gifts for the task.

The style of the book is anecdotal, autobiographical, and reflective rather than systematic or "academic." *The Buggies Still Run* will be, and deserves to be, widely read. Two categories of readers immediately come to mind—persons looking in on the "plain people," wondering what they are all about, and persons born into the tradition but baffled as to what to do with it. Rich as these pages are in theological and contemporary church topics, an index is a desideratum. Kissinger's recollections from his conscientious objector days (World War II) and discussion of nonresistance/pacifist issues should be readily available to a generation deciding what to do about registration. But then occupying a key post in the Library of Congress, Kissinger may be able to classify the book in such a way that it will surface under many topics.

I am left with questions, of course; a book that doesn't leave one thus is hardly worth reading. Kissinger draws on the classics of Troeltsch and (H. Richard) Niebuhr for a discussion of the church/sect issues. The latter was one of Kissinger's teachers at Yale. Niebuhr's *Christ and Culture,* variously echoed throughout Kissinger's monograph, is still widely read in undergraduate religion courses today. But some further things have been written on the theme since then that could well have been taken into account. Similarly, I am not fully comfortable with Kissinger's treatment of the nonresistance/pacifism debate. But then, for a Mennonite to comment on a Brethren treatment, what else can be expected?

Finally, I miss an adequate focus in Kissinger's treatment on the tension between the "charter" of the original radical Reformation movements and the folk culture which was meanwhile grown up around it. Perhaps he will try his hand at that in another volume. Meanwhile you may want to take your copy of *The Buggies Still Run,* drive to Dutch country, rent a horse and buggy, on a lazy afternoon, and as the horse ambles, curl up with the book.

Paul Peachey
Catholic University of America
Washington, D.C.

Preface

In my work as a subject cataloger at the Library of Congress, my prime objective in examining a book is to determine its subject content. In a word, what is the book about? As for the book in hand, it ranges over numerous subject areas. My basic intention has been to focus on the so-called "plain people" who are most numerous in Lancaster County, Pennsylvania, and to raise a number of issues which are more or less unique with them, but which also have a wider relevance. Since my own roots are in this tradition, my observations and reflections are positive, but also critical. They might best be categorized as being sympathetically-critical. Portions of the book relate experiences and make reflections on growing up in a small Pennsylvania Dutch community. I attempt to look at a tradition and a heritage and to ask what insights and guidance it has for the present and the future.

Chapter 1, which consists of a description and travel account of Lancaster County and an introduction to the plain people who live there, is followed by a discussion of various problems and characteristics which related to the plain tradition. Treated are such subjects as the simple life, nonresistance and pacifism, the experience of community, and the ethical dilemma posed by the growing and processing of cigar tobacco. The final chapter examines the heritage and transition of a small community in the heart of Lancaster County, the author's home town of Akron, Pennsylvania. Some concluding thoughts summarize the contributions of the plain people to our American culture.

In the 12th chapter of Hebrews, the writer speaks of being surrounded by a "great cloud of witnesses." He of course is referring to the witnesses of faith whom he had recounted in the preceeding chapter. I was aware of this imagery as I attempted to reflect upon my heritage and my pilgrimage. Each of us is surrounded by a great cloud of witnesses, both living and departed: parents, grandparents, siblings, teachers, ministers, neighbors, spouses, friends, scholars, writers, poets, artists, and musicians. In obvious ways and in ways not readily discernible, we have been and are surrounded by those who have influenced and shaped our thought, our perspective, our lives. Without them this book would not have been possible, and I take this opportunity to thank that "great cloud of witnesses" who have encouraged, inspired, and instructed me.

Warren S. Kissinger
University Park, Md.

1

Lancaster County
and the Plain People

There are several counties in the United States that for one reason or another are so well known that it is not necessary to identify them by the state in which they are located. One of them is Lancaster County. The city of Lancaster, the county seat of Lancaster County, is an important commercial and industrial center, and some of the largest stockyards in the East are located there. It was the home of James Buchanan, the 15th President of the United States. Among the educational institutions in Lancaster are Franklin and Marshall College, Lancaster Theological Seminary, and Thaddeus Stevens Industrial School for orphan boys. The Continental Congress met in Lancaster in 1777. During the 18th century the Conestoga wagon and the Pennsylvania rifle, both of which were significant for early American history, were produced there. Lancaster was the western terminus of the Lancaster Turnpike running from Philadelphia. This was the first macadamized highway in the United States, built between 1791 and 1797. From 1799 to 1812 Lancaster was the capital of Pennsylvania. But there are at least two other reasons for Lancaster County's fame. One is its agriculture, the other its "plain people."

Lancaster County's soil is highly fertile and productivity is probably higher than any non-irrigated area of the country. The limestone soil is particularly conducive to the growing of tobacco which has been the leading cash crop. The topography consists of gently rolling land which affords some pleasing vistas. Another important factor is the climate. Average annual temperature is 53 degrees, with annual rainfall of about 41 inches. The average growing season is 160 days long. Besides tobacco, other major crops are corn, wheat, and hay. Poultry and egg production, dairying, and beef cattle are also significant. In comparison with the national average, Lancaster County's farms are relatively small, averaging about 80 acres.

Lancaster's marketing potential is greatly enhanced by its proximity to major eastern metropolitan centers. It is 64 miles from Philadelphia, 67 miles from Baltimore, 106 miles from Washington, D.C., 160 miles from New York City. Major highway and railroad facilities are additional assets. As one might expect, the city and county have numerous markets where local produce, baked goods, and handicrafts are marketed. A visit to one of Lancaster's markets is a unique experience. There one will see an abundance of meats, cheeses, baked products, including such favorites as snitz and shoo-fly pies, vegetables, flowers and plants, and much more. A familiar scene in Lancaster City is people carrying market baskets on market day. It is not difficult to understand why Lancaster County has often been referred to as the world's garden spot.

In more recent times, tourism has become one of Lancaster's prominent industries. And of course the farmers' markets are major attractions. Meadowbrook Farmers' Market, east of Lancaster, is perhaps the most prominent insofar as tourism is concerned. On any spring and summer Saturday, vast bus loads of tourists from the eastern metropolitan centers visit Meadowbrook. The crowds are so large at times that it is difficult to thread one's way through the market. Attached to the market is a country store and a flea market which sell clothing, crafts, and antiques. Meadowbrook is a newer market than some of the others. Consequently, it has an antiseptic quality and lacks the rusticity of some of the older ones. My favorite is Green Dragon which is located just northeast of Ephrata. The "dragon comes alive" every Friday, and in addition to the usual market fare there are auction sales of livestock, hay and straw, and dry goods. To spend some time at the livestock auction is to "savor the flavor" of the Pennsylvania Dutch community. Although Green Dragon has been enlarged recently and has become more gaudy, there is still an unspoiled quality about it. And if one looks and listens sensitively, one can discern something of the essence and the genius of the Pennsylvania Dutch culture. During the 1976 Bicentennial activities in Washington, D.C., there was a strong emphasis on the American ethnic communities and their contribution to the American ethos. I had the opportunity of discussing the

14

Pennsylvania Dutch community with a noted folklorist who was very familiar with the area. She concurred that Green Dragon was an excellent place for gaining insights about the Pennsylvania Dutch.

About one half mile south of Lititz on the way to Lancaster is the small village of Kissel Hill. There a family named Stauffer started a roadside market in 1935. Today "Stauffer's of Kissel Hill" has four locations in Lancaster County and has grown into a rather unique institution. I am most familiar with the original Kissel Hill location. There is a veritable cornucopia of local produce and meats as well as an impressive array of citrus and tropical fruits. Stauffer's features a garden center with flowers, plants, and everything for the garden. Flower workshops and flower-arranging classes, which attract local as well as out-of-town participants lend an artistic and creative dimension. While Stauffer's of Kissel Hill has a wide-ranging, even prolific, array of merchandise, a tasteful and subdued quality makes it most pleasing and attractive.

In addition to the large public farmers' markets there are the roadside stands which are most intriguing. These are operated by individual farm families and feature produce and articles grown, baked, and made by them. During the late spring and summer months, it is a real joy to stop by one or more of these stands, not only to see and buy what is being sold, but also to converse with the people—to share as it were, if only for a brief moment, their joys and concerns, their problems and aspirations. Such brief encounters are often more meaningful than hours spent at some of the garish tourist "hot spots" which for a "reasonable fee" introduce you to things Pennsylvania Dutch.

If one is in Lancaster County on a Monday, a visit to the horse auction at New Holland affords a good opportunity to observe an institution which has been in operation for many years. The Amish and Old Order Mennonites rely on the auction for their horses. Many of the horses, however, are sold to foreign buyers (particularly French) and are shipped abroad to be slaughtered and used for human consumption. In addition to the horse sale, hogs also are auctioned on Mondays. On Wednesdays there is a dairy cattle sale, and on Thursdays beef cattle are sold.

At New Holland the distinctions between sect and world are minimized, except for the differences in attire. There is an intriguing paradox here, and perhaps a harsh judgment upon

15

the church. Christianity has been marked by a divisiveness that prevents fellowship among Christians from being easy or natural. Our theologies and traditions divide us rather than unite us. But in the marketplace a unanimity of ideology and purpose prevails and nurtures a sense of community which transcends racial, religious, and class distinctions. Maybe Jesus had something of this in mind when, after telling the parable of the Unjust Steward, he observed that the children of this world are wiser in their own generation than the children of light (Luke 16:8).

Lancaster County's renowned agricultural production and its so-called plain people are inseparable. Today the vast majority of Lancaster's farming community consists of members of the plain sect. They are the Amish, the Mennonites, the Brethren, and the Brethren in Christ. The Mennonites were among the earliest settlers in Lancaster County and they may have represented the first European group settlement. They arrived in Lancaster around 1710. The oldest known building in the county is the Hans Herr House near Willow Street. It was used both as a residence and a place of worship and was built by Christian Herr for his father, Hans Herr, who was the bishop of the original Mennonite settlement. Lancaster County has the largest concentration of Mennonites and Amish of any area of the United States.

It is quite common to equate the Pennsylvania Dutch with the plain people. They are, however, a minority of Lancaster County's population. Besides the plain people or the plain sects, the majority of the population comprise the "gay" or "fancy" Dutch, many of whom come out of the Lutheran and Reformed traditions. One uses the word "gay" with some apprehension today because it has become so widely identified with homosexuality. But "gay" and "fancy" with reference to the Pennsylvania Dutch imply that they comply more closely with the prevailing culture than do the "plain" Dutch. In a word, they are more "worldly" than their plain neighbors. Throughout the years Lancaster County has represented a unique juxtaposition of "plain and fancy," of sect and church.

A word should be said about the terms "Pennsylvania Dutch" and "Pennsylvania German." The Pennsylvania Dutch word for "German" is *deitsch* which has a close resemblance to "Dutch." Thus "Pennsylvania Dutch" may be a corruption of "Pennsylvania deitsch." The Pennsylvania deitsch became known as the Pennsylvania Dutch. The Pennsylvania Dutch

16

dialect, however, does not originate from Holland Dutch but is rather a *Plattdeutsch,* a low German, which today still has a close resemblance to the dialect spoken in the Palatinate region of Germany. It is thus more precise to speak of the ethnic group as the Pennsylvania Dutch, while referring to their dialect as Pennsylvania German. Recently the Library of Congress (LOC) has changed its subject headings to conform to this distinction. The LOC catalogers originally used "Pennsylvania Dutch" to refer to the dialect as well as the people. Henceforth, "Pennsylvania German" will be the subject heading for the language and "Pennsylvania Dutch" the subject heading for the ethnic group.

The religious milieu of Lancaster County affords a fertile field of study for the religious sociologist. It is a dynamic microcosm for the observation and analysis of the phenomenon known by social scientists as acculturation. It was Ernst Troeltsch who brought to the foreground of religious sociology the typology of "church" and "sect" and their dichotomy. He described the church type as that organization which is overwhelmingly conservative because to a degree it accepts the secular order and tends toward universality, desiring to cover the whole life of humanity. The church type accommodates the existing social order more readily than does the sect type. It becomes a stabilizing and determinant dimension of the social order.

The church type is exemplified by the state churches of Europe and to a lesser degree by the so-called mainline churches in the United States. The "plain people," especially the Old Order Amish, are classic examples of Troeltsch's sect type. In Lancaster County, these distinctions were and still are evident in the differing religious and cultural stance reflected by the plain people or the plain sects, and the "gay" or "fancy" Dutch, such as members of the Lutheran and the Reformed churches.

The stance of the sect type is quite different from that of the church type. The sects may be indifferent, tolerant, or many times hostile toward the state and society. They have no desire to incorporate or control the prevailing forms of social life. Instead they tend to avoid them or even to replace these social institutions with their own society. The sects tend to take the Sermon on the Mount as their ideal and insist on a radical opposition between the Kingdom of God and all secular interests and institutions. They want to return to the "purity" of primitive Christianity, and they accuse the church of having

17

fallen away from its ideal, of having become "unequally yoked together with unbelievers," and of having renounced noncomformity with the world. "Be not conformed to this world" and "Do not love the world or the things in the world" are clarion challenges of the sects.

The distinction between church and sect is perhaps most dramatically set forth in their respective views of the sacraments, particularly baptism and church membership. The church is universal and inclusive and has an objective institutional character. Thus, the individual is born into the church and through infant baptism comes under its miraculous influence. The sectarian pattern is quite otherwise. The sect is a voluntary community whose members join it of their own free will. One is not born into the sect but enters it on the basis of conscious conversion. For the sects, infant baptism is a stumbling block. One must "repent and be baptized"; not infant baptism, but "believers' baptism" is the authentic and biblical pattern according to the sects. Church membership entails a moral discipline, a sort of "worldly asceticism" which places more emphasis upon the quality of one's life than the correctness of one's theology. It is the sects which have insisted upon and nurtured such qualities as simplicity, service, fellowship, peace, nonswearing, family life, spirituality, and discipleship. While the sects regard Jesus as Savior and Lord, they also are captivated by his example and his style of life. They have been more concerned with *Nachfolge* (discipleship, following after Jesus) than with the niceties and entanglements of christological formulations.

In addition to Troeltsch, H. Richard Niebuhr has dealt with the church-sect distinction with his Christ and culture typology. The relationship between Christianity and civilization, between the Christian and culture, can be stated in five categories. These are: Christ against culture, the Christ of culture, Christ above culture, Christ and culture in paradox, and Christ the transformer of culture. For our purposes we are interested primarily in the Christ against culture position, since this corresponds closely to Troeltsch's sect-type. The Christ against culture stance uncompromisingly affirms the sole authority of Christ over the Christian and resolutely rejects culture's claims to loyalty. Niebuhr observes that the Mennonites have come to represent the attitude most purely, since their traditional position has been to renounce all participation in politics and they have consistently refused to be drawn into military service. Moreover, they follow their own distinctive customs and regulations in economics and education.

From the foregoing analysis it is apparent that Lancaster County's plain people are classic examples of Troeltsch's sect-type and Niebuhr's Christ against culture position. But even for the radical sectarians, culture is an ever-present reality and "threat." This leads us to some observations about the plain people and their response to their cultural context.

Among the plain people it is the Mennonites, and particularly the Old Order Amish, who maintain the most radical stance toward the prevailing culture. As noted above, the Mennonites were among the first Europeans to arrive in Lancaster County. They were representative of a movement stemming from the Protestant Reformation in the sixteenth century. A small group of Swiss Brethren felt that the existing churches did not meet biblical standards and the spiritual needs of the people. They felt that the Reformation had been a halfway response and needed to go further. Consequently, the Anabaptists, as the Swiss Brethren were later called, are often referred to as the radical reformers, or their movement is spoken of as the left wing of the Reformation. They contended for a free church which was not established by and connected with the state. They rejected infant baptism and instituted adult believers' baptism.

Those who voluntarily joined the group were expected to live a life marked by discipline and discipleship to Christ. In the Bible, and particularly in the Sermon on the Mount, one had a guide and source for Christian life and conduct. They believed that the church was a community, a fellowship, governed by love and truth. For them, war and killing were contrary to the spirit, the life, and the teachings of Jesus whom they saw as their guide and example. As one of the early Anabaptists professed: "To know Christ truly is to follow him daily in life." As might be expected, the Anabaptists encountered hardship and persecution, and they became scattered throughout Europe. Some migrated to America and since the latter part of the seventeenth century they have been a small but significant part of the American community.

The Amish, who generally receive more attention and publicity than the Mennonites, are a part of the Anabaptist movement. They take their name from Jacob Ammon, a Swiss (Bernese) Mennonite bishop of the late seventeenth century. Ammon insisted upon a stricter adherence to the confession of faith than he believed the Mennonites were following. He especially was insistent upon enforcing the ban, the expulsion of disobedient members from the fellowship. Those who agreed with Ammon's more conservative stance joined with him in founding a new movement. Later Ammon's group migrated to Pennsylvania, and today the largest concentration of Amish are to be found in Lancaster County.

Another segment of the plain people comes out of the Brethren movement originally known as German Baptist Brethren. They had their origin in Germany in the early years of the eighteenth century and were strongly influenced by German pietism. Their affinities with the Anabaptists are also unmistakable. The Brethren migrated to Pennsylvania soon after their origin and subsequently became entirely an American church.

Lancaster County has one of the largest populations of Brethren in the United States. The process of acculturation among Lancaster County plain people is more advanced among the Brethren than among the Amish and the Mennonites. They have been moving off the farms and entering other means of occupation far more readily than their Anabaptist counterparts. Another evidence of these differences is the Brethren participation (unlike the Amish and the Mennonites) in the ecumenical and conciliar movements. The plain dress, which is still rigidly adhered to by the Amish and the Old Order Mennonites, has been to a large extent abandoned by the Brethren.

Another group which traditionally has been identified with the plain people is the River Brethren or Brethren in Christ. It is a relatively small group in Lancaster County and like the Brethren, some of their "peculiar" practices are giving way to the onrush of modernity. The Brethren in Christ have cooperated with the Mennonites in peace and service programs.

The problem of the relation of Christ to culture and particularly the stance of Christ against culture comes to its sharpest focus in Lancaster County among the Amish and the Old Order Mennonites. By "Old Order Mennonites" I refer to those groups who use horse and buggies for transportation and who use German and Pennsylvania German in their worship services.

The threat of the world or the culture for the radical sectarians is evident in various ways. Perhaps the most dramatic encounter in recent years between "Christ and culture" in Lancaster County has been the long struggle between the Amish and public education. The Amish have consistently and vociferously objected to their children attending high school. They have maintained their one-room schoolhouses and have insisted that an eighth-grade education is sufficient.

Traditionally the Amish have engaged almost exclusively in farming or related occupations. It is no secret that they have been among the most adept and successful agriculturalists in the country. Their care and cultivation of the soil is ingrained in their religious convictions. They are stewards of God's creation. Nature is to be cared for so that what is passed on to others is as good or better than when it was received. The Amish have adhered to this legacy and today the productiveness of their farms is as high or higher than it was when their forebears arrived many years ago.

It is likewise no secret that Amish women are quite expert in homemaking. If the quality of their cooking or their ability to make clothing and quilts is the standard, then they rank among the best of our home economists.

These arts of tending the soil and managing the household have been and are passed on to each generation with father teaching son and mother teaching daughter. The Amish insist that higher education is not necessary for them to further their way of life. Their ideal is to maintain their communities within traditional boundaries, and they correctly discern that higher education would expose their children to "worldly influences" which would slowly but surely erode their traditions.

Attendance at high school would require the busing of Amish children away from their local one-room schools to large, distant consolidated schools. There they would be introduced to an education which goes beyond the basics of reading, writing, and arithmetic which they regard as sufficient for the propagation of their way of life. Their interest is not in reforming the public education system. They are not in the vanguard of the "back to basics" movement. Indeed they need "educated" people in their communities because they rely on outside teachers (particularly Mennonites) to teach their children. They consult physicians when they are ill. On rare occasions, particularly in the school struggle, they have had to rely upon the aid of lawyers. They are not anti-education, rather they want to be "left alone" so that they can perpetuate their traditions and their way of life. Parenthetically, in a day

21

of increasing scarcity, reduced standards of living, pollution of air and water, crime, violence, shoddy workmanship, disintegrating family life, the Amish way increasingly appears attractive.

The long struggle between the Amish and the state of Pennsylvania concerning high school education has now been resolved. Amish children of high school age are required to attend an Amish vocational school for three hours a week during which time they are taught such subjects as English, mathematics, health, and social studies by an Amish teacher. For the balance of the week, the children perform farm and household duties under parental supervision and keep a journal of their daily activities. The major portion of the curriculum consists of home projects in agriculture and homemaking. Thus, an issue replete with knotty problems on the relationship between church and state, of individual rights and societal responsibility, of "unequal" justice, has been resolved. It seems like a prudent and sensible solution, although it is still unsatisfactory for the legal "purists."

Besides education, the encroachment of the "world" upon the sects is evident in other areas. The rapid growth of industrialization and of the population represents serious threats to sectarian Christianity. Today Lancaster City is a significant industrial and commercial center and the surrounding area has grown rapidly. Between 1969 and 1970 Lancaster County had an increase of 25 percent in its urban population, and by all indications this growth is continuing apace. This means that more and more land which was once used for agriculture is now being "developed." The city is spreading and engulfing more and more choice farmland. What was yesterday "open country," today may be occupied by shopping malls, industries, and highways. For the plain people, this means that increasingly there is less land available for farming. With their relatively large families it is impossible to give each of the sons a farm as was once the custom. Consequently, many Amish and Old Order Mennonites must engage in work which removes them one step farther from the farm and increases the potential of exposure to worldliness, One solution, at least for many Amish, has been migration. Through the years, groups of Amish have migrated from Lancaster County to other parts of the state and to other states where land was cheaper and where there was more "breathing space."

The cost of land has become a monumental problem. An

Amishman told me recently that prime land is now selling around $5,000 per acre. With the prevailing high interest rates it virtually is impossible to buy a farm and to hope to make much of a profit. In order to preserve their communities and to "keep out the developers," the plain people are forced to pay exorbitant prices for land. This situation poses for the sectarians an ominous and uncertain future.

Industrialization and growth of course bring new people into a community. This results in a movement from homogeneity to heterogeneity, from isolationism to cosmopolitanism. New people bring with them different cultural mores, values, and lifestyles. The staid Pennsylvania Dutch culture is increasingly being exposed to Spanish Americans, blacks, asiatics, and New England Yankees, and the resulting "melting pot" is bound to produce a different community than what it was before. Today the once-isolated Pennsylvania Dutch cultural islands are being exposed to new forces which tend to erode their distinctiveness. I discern in the Pennsylvania Dutch a sense of self-identity and pride which will make cultural amalgamation a painful and perhaps traumatic experience. I used to hear it said by some who were not overawed by their Army experience that there is a right way to do things and then there is the Army way. That stance suits the Pennsylvania Dutch. By their thoughts, if not their actions, one soon discerns that there is a right way to do things, and that of course is the Pennsylvania Dutch way. There is a right way to farm, to cook, to clean house, to live, and then there are other ways which are seemingly innately inferior.

How the Pennsylvania Dutch will adjust to different cultural influences in their midst remains to be seen. The implications for the survival of the plain people are crucial. Roland Bainton, the Yale church historian who is most sympathetic with the sects, used to point out that the sects are destroyed not by persecution but by fraternization with the world. What fire, dungeon, sword, and drowning could not do, the subtle "friendliness with the world" can do—erode the sectarian witness and blur the distinction and the tension between "Christ and culture."

For the Amish particularly, the demands of culture by way of state requirements have necessitated some accomodation. This was true with the education issue but also with their dairying practices. Some years ago the state of Pennsylvania required the use of bulk tanks for storing milk. This meant not

23

only the purchase of new equipment, but the more basic consideration of a power source. Since Amish farms are not equipped with electricity, milking had been done by hand. But with the advent of milking machines and bulk tanks some type of power was required. Electricity is still prohibited, but diesel engines are used to operate the dairy equipment. The milk is picked up by tank truck every other day, Sunday excluded. As one goes through the Amish area, one notices the absence of telephone and electric wires and the presence of windmills. Water is pumped by windmills or, if a stream flows through the farm, by water wheels.

Another subtle problem involves the purchase of a farm where electrical power is already installed. In former times, the electrical wiring had to be removed. Today the situation is more ambiguous. There may be a period of "grace" during which electricity is used and later dispensed with. Or the family may continue to use the electricity since it was not installed by them but was there when they moved in. Here again, what may appear to outsiders as trivial and nitpicking, for the Amish are vital issues. For they know, as all of us must, that "worldliness" does not appear suddenly and full-blown, but slowly, subtly, ingeniously. For the Amish and the Old Order Mennonites the biblical figure of the devil as an angel of light has become literal as well as figurative.

Modern technology has put another stumbling block and enticement before Amish youth particularly. That temptation is the battery-powered transistor radio. There was a day when most radios were rather large and cumbersome and required an electrical outlet for a power source. But with batteries and the replacement of vacuum tubes with transistors, radios have become more compact and portable. Consequently, radios have become standard fare in the buggies of many youth. On a summer evening, or winter evening for that matter, one may hear strange sounds emanating from a buggy—sounds which come neither from horse or riders, but from such "worldly" centers as Broadway and Hollywood.

One of the most notable changes in Lancaster County in the past 50 years has been the advent and growth of tourism and the tourist industry. Sadly, the Amish have borne the brunt of this development. They have been the "drawing card" for tourists who have been coming in increasing numbers from all parts of the country. As noted earlier, Lancaster is in close proximity to the large eastern metropolitan areas. The "Dutch country" is an easy day's excursion for many urbanites, and others as well. What were once narrow, pastoral byways, traversed by buggies and an occasional automobile, now have become major tour bus routes. The attempted isolation by the Amish is continuously being violated by those who come to "gawk" and to take pictures which the Amish object to. The Amish consider "graven images" prohibited by the Ten Commandments.

One must wonder about the reasons for this preoccupation with the Amish. Does the attraction lie in the fact that here are "peculiar people" who *are* different from our mass, conformist society? In a society where individuality is discouraged and where most of us experience a crisis of self-identity, are we mysteriously drawn toward people who know who they are, what they believe, and who *are* "doing their own thing?" Or maybe there is the romantic and utopian in each of us which longs for a simpler and less hectic existence than is now experienced. Perhaps it is our way of vicariously regressing to the "good old days." At any rate, tourism is a reality (some would say a harsh and garish reality) in Lancaster County.

The tourist boom is most glaringly evident along Route 30 east of Lancaster. It has almost come to resemble a miniaturized Las Vegas strip replete with motels, restaurants, shops, and amusement centers, many of which feature "Amish stuff." The Old Philadelphia Pike which leads from Lancaster to Intercourse and goes through the Amish area is fast being "developed" and coming to have some of the same objectionable elements as Route 30.

It is offensive to one's sense of propriety, to say the least, when one is directed to visit such places as the Amish Country Golf Course, the Amish Hat Gift Shop, the Dutch Wagon Wheel, Dutch Wonderland, and so on and on. In a recent visit to a restaurant in Lancaster County, I was intrigued to see Amish dolls which were made in Long Island City, N.Y. I'm sure some would be made in Taiwan and Hong Kong. In front of one of Lancaster County's finest diners stands a gigantic replica of an Amishman. His name is Amos and he "talks" to patrons as they enter the diner. The diner serves excellent Pennsylvania Dutch food and is to be highly recommended. However, it is removed from the Amish area of the country by quite a number of miles. It is but one more evidence of the exploitation of the Amish for the sake of the tourist trade. Perhaps it is not only the scarcity of land that has caused many

Amish to migrate but also the "oppression" of the tourist industry. Surely some of them must envision an area for living which has not yet been discovered by tourists. So the struggle between "Christ and culture" persists in subtle and not so subtle ways.

There are a few notable exceptions to this blatant exploitation of the plain people in the cause of mammon. The Mennonites have taken the initiative to interpret their faith and way of life to outsiders. East of Lancaster, just south of the Lincoln Highway on Millstream Road, is the Mennonite Information Center. Anyone wanting authentic information about the Amish and the Mennonites and an introduction to the Pennsylvania Dutch country should by all means make a visit to the Information Center. The Center, established in 1961, specializes in providing services to tourists and to researchers interested in Mennonite and Amish culture. A film, "The Mennonite Story," features a Mennonite family at home on their farm in Lancaster County. The Center also features literature and displays pertaining to the Amish and Mennonites.

From the Information Center one can go on a guided tour through the Amish and Mennonite farmlands. The guides are all local Mennonites who know the area and the people. One is introduced to Mennonite churches, one-room Amish schools, historic sites, Mennonite and/or Amish farms, Amish crafts, an Amish cemetery, a coach shop, and others.

Perhaps the most impressive feature of the Mennonite Information Center is the Library and the Archives. It has frequently been pointed out that there is no religious group which has done a more thorough research of its historical resources than have the Mennonites. The scope and operation of the Library and the Archives are significant evidence of this claim. The Library focuses upon three basic services: historical research, genealogical research, and theological research. The Library contains approximately 40,000 theological books plus about 20,000 historical and genealogical books. Acquisitions continue at a fast pace and, as with most libraries, space is a major factor. In all probability, expansion of the Library's facilities will be necessary in the not too distant future.

The Library's historical materials concentrate on Mennonite and Amish items but also include a large collection of histories related to southeastern Pennsylvania denominations that tie in with the early Mennonite history of the area. It collects local history to provide the larger contextual background for Mennonite-related history.

The Library's most extensively used service is that of genealogical research. Here there is a wealth of material exceeded by few institutions in the United States. Consequently, researchers from all over the United States, Canada, and even Europe, visit the Library every year. The central feature of the genealogical research area is a card file of over 200,000 cards containing names, dates, and other vital statistics. Additional genealogical resources include census records, cemetery records, deed abstracts, will abstracts, and local newspapers. Many of the Lancaster County cemeteries, as well as many cemeteries in surrounding counties, have been transcribed, and the Library has a cemetery index.

The Lancaster Mennonite Historical Society which administers the Library serves as the official depository for archival records of all Lancaster Mennonite Conference ordained leaders, committees, and congregations, and it also serves other conferences and committees within the geographic region. The archives include diaries, correspondence, deeds, church bulletins, programs, record books, and photographs.

Among the many other activities and services of the Mennonite Information Center are the book auctions which are held bimonthly. Persons having books for sale consign them for the auction and subsequently receive a certain percentage of the sale price. The staff and volunteers at the Information Center process and sort the books. They write descriptions and conditions and mail mimeographed lists of the books to prospective buyers. In 1978, over 700 such lists were mailed. Those who cannot attend the auctions can submit mail bids prior to the sale by consulting these lists. Attendance at the book auctions may range from 50 to 100 persons. In addition to the general run of books, an occasional rare item such as an Ephrata Community imprint may invoke spirited interest and bidding.

Another authentic source of information about Lancaster County's Amish and Mennonite communities is The People's Place at Intercourse. The prominent emphasis is on Amish and Mennonite arts and crafts, and exhibits by Mennonite, Amish, and Hutterite artists and photographers are featured. The People's Place has one of the widest selections of books about Mennonite, Amish, and Hutterite identity, history, faith, and culture. The Amish Story Museum comprises a collection of unique three-dimensional carved paintings by Aaron Zook, a local Amishman, which reflect an insider's view of Amish culture. Among the activities depicted are a barn-raising, springtime plowing, the farmer's market, an Amish wedding, a one-room school, the Sunday service, death in the community, and "The Father's Evening Prayer." These are scenes which are seldom seen by most Americans but which take on a lifelike quality thanks to Amish craftsman Aaron Zook. In the midst of the rampant commercial exploitation of the Amish and the Mennonites, The People's Place is a haven characterized by integrity, authenticity, and sensitivity.

Returning to the process of acculturation among the plain people, noticeable shifts and movements within and among the various groups have been evident across the years. The radical stance of Christ against culture has been marked to a great extent by visible forms and a strict adherence to rules and cultural peculiarities. These practices at times have been invested with ecclesiastical and even divine authority. The plain people in their struggle with acculturation have invariably interpreted "worldliness" in terms of fashionable clothing and modern conveniences and means of communication and transportation such as electricity, automobiles, farm machinery, telephones, radios, televisions. Consequently, rules were formulated which attempted to prescribe what was permissable and what was prohibited. Given the constant flux and imminent change that attend culture and technology, this response is fraught with monumental dilemmas. Today there are as many as 20 Mennonite groups as well as a number of Amish ones. These divisions represent the perennial "search for purity" on the part of the plain people. Many of the divisions have centered around such areas as church architecture, plain dress versus "worldly dress," horse and buggies versus automobiles. The attempt to legislate and to define what a Christian disciple should be and do has always been a central problem for Christian ethics, and it especially is so for the plain people. Those outside the sectarian community are often quick to criticize what they consider to be legalism, inconsistency, and spiritual pride. These issues will be discussed in a later chapter.

As noted above, there has not only been a marked fragmentation of the plain people but also significant movement from one group to another, and this is evidence of a sort of acculturation. For example, certain Old Order Mennonites or Amish may come to disagree with the community's prohibition of automobiles and they may subsequently join a group where automobiles are permitted. One group of Mennonites—the

Hornung Mennonites—are allowed to have automobiles provided they are second-hand and the chromium is painted black. They have been referred to colloquially as the "black-bumper Mennonites." While their vehicles are motorized, peculiarity and separation are still maintained by virture of their all-black cars. They provide a plausible alternative for those of the Old Order who welcome automobiles but who still want to maintain their unique identity.

Most of the Old Order Mennonites allow the use of tractors for farm work provided the wheels are steel rather than rubber. Here is another alternative for those who use horses for transportation but who find tractors more efficient for drawing farm equipment.

In a conversation with a Lancaster Conference Mennonite, I was informed that in recent years a number of Hornung Mennonites came into the Lancaster Conference because they wanted their children to receive a Christian education in Sunday school, an option not open to them since the Hornung group has no Sunday school program.

The Lancaster Conference and the General Conference Mennonites are among the most progressive in the use of modern conveniences and transportation. In dress there is variation from plain to "fancy," with a discernible movement toward the latter. The struggle for uniformity, order and consistency is one which has proved distressingly illusive for the plain people.

As for the Brethren and the Brethren in Christ, they have abandoned the outward signs of nonconformity to a greater extent than have the Mennonites. There are still some exceptions, especially in reference to plain dress. The process of acculturation, the movement from sect-type to church-type, from "Christ against culture" to the "Christ of culture" is most in evidence among the Brethren. From a background very similar to that of the Mennonites, they have been a kind of bridge between the sectarian and churchly traditions. Thus, they have been affiliated with the National and the World Councils of Churches and have been active in local and state conciliar movements. This has produced something of an identity crisis among the Brethren, and the cleavages between sectarian and churchly, between conservative and liberal views are persistent issues.

In this process of movement among and within the plain people, the Brethren have often been viewed as the end of the continuum. Across the years quite a number of Mennonites have joined the Brethren, some because of marriage, but others because the Brethren represented a more liberal and open stance while still maintaining a semblance of the ideal of nonconformity.

Among the historical developments related to the plain people, perhaps none is more unique than the Ephrata Community. The founder and leader of the Ephrata Community, until his death in 1768, was Johann Conrad Beissel. He was an exile from the Rhenish Palatinate who arrived in Germantown in 1720. It was there that Beissel became associated with the Dunkers, or German Baptists, or Brethren as they were later called. Peter Becker, who led the first migration of Brethren from Europe to America in 1719, was a weaver, and he accepted Beissel as an apprentice.

In the fall of 1723, Beissel and a group of Brethren made a long missionary journey which brought them into Conestoga, an area which is now a part of Lancaster County. Here he followed his original intention to live the life of a hermit. Finally, after considerable deliberation, Beissel consented to baptism and was immersed by Becker. Thus, he became a member of the Brethren group, and for seven years he was head of the new congregation in Conestoga. Under Beissel's leadership the relationship between Conestoga and Germantown grew strained, and it finally ended in schism.

The contention between Beissel and the Germantown Brethren centered around three issues. He was attracted to certain Judaistic doctrines and customs, chief of which was the observance of the seventh day as the Sabbath. Secondly, he scorned marriage and preached the superiority of celibacy. And, finally, he proselytized in areas where the Germantown Brethren regarded themselves as the rightful owners. It was Beissel's Sabbatarianism which became the principal outward point of difference between his group and the Brethren.

Toward the end of 1728, Beissel determined to separate himself from the Germantown Brethren. He suddenly gave up his office as elder of the Conestoga congregation and departed once more to the wilderness and the solitary life. This time he went to Ephrata on the Cocalico Creek and took shelter in the hut of an Alsatian hermit, Emmanuel Eckerling. Soon others joined the Ephrata settlement and converts began arriving from various points. They erected convents and chapels on Mount Zion (the hill rising above the Cocalico) and other buildings in the meadow at the base of the hill. Eventually this settlement of Seventh-day German Baptists grew to include three semi-independent orders living in close cooperation — a brotherhood, a sisterhood, and a congregation of married couples or "householders."

Ephrata thus became one of the most unique communities in colonial America. Visitors came from far and near. It was not only a noted religious community but it was also a leading printing center. In addition, it was famous for its music. Music was written and published, and there were also singing schools. The Brotherhood was self-sustaining. The members engaged in farming and orcharding. They practiced such handicrafts as shoemaking, tailoring, and weaving cloth and stockings. They had bakeries, and their bread was of outstanding quality.

The greatest practical achievement of the Community was the establishment and the operation of a series of mills. These included a gristmill, a sawmill, a flaxseed-oil mill, and a fulling mill, and from these came the paper and the ink used in their printing. They also set up a tannery, as well as looms for weaving woolen and linen cloth.

The Brotherhood had at least one significant relationship with the American Revolution. Following the battle of Brandywine, the large buildings on Zion Hill were taken over as a military hospital for the patriot troops. Here members of the community nursed and cared for the wounded. The soldiers who died were buried on Zion Hill, and an obelisk marks their burial place.

In addition to their printing, the Ephrata Community produced illuminated manuscripts and *Frakturschriften*. They revived the medieval art of illumination and raised it to a high point of excellence. At first this work was begun to provide manuscripts for the Cloister choirs, but later a mystical significance appears to have been attached to it and it was pursued as a spiritual exercise. Each brother or sister, instructed to work under divine inspiration, produced designs of forceful vigor and delicate loveliness, rich in mystic significance. Today faded fragments still hang on the walls of the Saal in Ephrata. Formerly, the whole interior of the convent was decorated with such pieces, many of them memorials to the dead. Because of their value as collectors' items, these manuscripts have been widely dispersed.

Without a doubt, the most extensive and significant enterprise of the Ephrata Community centered around the printing press. Between 1745 and 1794, the Cloister Press printed an amazing amount and diversity of material. Much of the work was written at Ephrata and was generally of a devotional character. Other work was ordered from outside.

The most famous and by far the most laborious commission executed at the Ephrata Press was the printing of the Mennonite Book of Martyrs. This work was originally written in Low Dutch by Tielman Jans Van Bracht. The Mennonites wished to have it translated into German, and this was done by Peter Miller who succeeded Beissel as the leader of the Community. The work was translated, printed, and bound at Ephrata over a three-year period, and was completed in 1751. The title was *Der Blutige Schau-Platz oder Martyrer Spiegel der Tauffs Gesinten oder Wehrlosen-Christen*. It consisted of a compilation of biographical sketches relating the sufferings and the confessions of those martyrs who, since the apostolic age, were opposed to the baptism of infants and to warfare. The Mennonites believed that these confessions were inspired. The Book of Martyrs was to be found in many Mennonite homes and served as a constant reminder of the high cost of Christian discipleship.

The *Martyrer Spiegel,* containing 1,514 pages, was the largest work published in America in the eighteenth century. The edition, which was 1,300 copies, required 1,184 reams of extra-heavy paper, which came from the Ephrata mill. The binding was very substantial; it consisted of board covered with leather, with brass corners and clasps.

With the death of Beissel in 1768, Ephrata was never the same again. Gradually the Community declined and finally ceased to exist. The buildings were neglected and deteriorated badly. Those on the hill were destroyed by the ravages of time. The brothers' house also fell into decay and was finally torn down. Many valuable furnishings and artifacts were carried away. These conditions persisted until the Cloister was taken over by the state of Pennsylvania. The buildings which remained were restored, and today the Ephrata Cloister is a noted tourist attraction, visited by thousands of people each year.

Today the Ephrata Cloister is a museum. The varied activities, the spiritual exercises, and all the achievements, as well as the foibles of those who came and went and lived there, have long since ceased. As one passes through the narrow passages, stands in the many rooms, and strolls the surrounding grounds, one can imagine only dimly the life that once flourished there. To visit Ephrata is to be transferred back to an era that "progress" has starkly replaced. The once-isolated residence of the Solitary in the wilderness is now surrounded by the trappings of contemporary culture—a shopping center, an industry, a cloverleaf, and housing developments. But a visit to Ephrata—this island of eighteenth-century monasticism surrounded by a sea of modernity—can still serve to remind us that one "does not live by bread alone, but by every word that proceeds from the mouth of God."

For the plain people, service to those in need has always been a central concern. In recent years several innovative projects are noteworthy. Both the Mennonites and the Brethren have developed self-help programs which are marketing outlets for skilled craftspersons in many developing countries around the world. The Mennonite Self-Help Program is an arm of the Mennonite Central Committee and is supported by the Mennonites and the Brethren in Christ. The headquarters and central shipping point for the program is located at Ephrata. However, retail outlets for Self-Help products are spread throughout Canada and the United States. A similar program operated by the Church of the Brethren, called SERRV, is based at the Church World Service Center in New Windsor, Maryland. SERRV also has numerous retail outlets throughout the country.

The goal of the Self-Help Program and of SERRV is to help people earn a living through their traditional crafts. They focus particularly on artisans who have very few other vocational opportunities because they live in poor countries and/or are refugees, handicapped persons, or members of a disadvantaged minority group.

A visit to a Self-Help Program or SERRV store is fascinating and informative. The shelves are full of brilliantly embroidered linens, hand-carved useful and decorative wood products, tooled leather, children's toys, clothing articles, and a vast array of crafts too numerous to mention. Unlike other "shopping centers," the proceeds from one's purchases go to assist some of those most in need.

At the same location in Ephrata as the Self-Help Program, the Mennonites operate a clothing processing center. Clothing, blankets, and quilts are processed and sent out to meet human need. Most of the work is done by volunteers who come daily to sort and bale clothing. The Amish are quite active in these projects and frequently come to Ephrata by hired buses in order to contribute a day's work.

The Church of the Brethren, in conjunction with Church World Service, operates a more extensive relief program at New Windsor, Maryland. In addition to processing clothing, the Center serves as a distribution point for drugs, medicines, and medical supplies which mostly are shipped abroad. Throughout its existence the New Windsor Center has also provided temporary shelter for refugees who were in the process of being relocated in the United States. More recently New Windsor has become a significant retreat and conference center, it entertains thousands of visitors each year.

To visit Ephrata and/or New Windsor is an experience not soon forgotten. Here are living, dynamic, creative attempts to serve, to seek to build rather than to destroy, to take seriously and act upon Jesus' admonition that as we do it to one of the least we do it unto him.

Another program which was inaugurated by the Mennonites and is now growing among the Brethren is meat canning. Periodically, meat and broth are canned and subsequently sent to disaster areas or other points of need both home and abroad. These projects involve not only sizable monetary contributions but also extensive volunteer labor. The Mennonite Central Committee operates a "Portable Meat Canner" which is transported on a 38-foot tractor trailer rig. The Canner moves from one community to another and is kept busy most of the year.

Besides meat products, the Mennonites and Brethren also have distributed other foodstuffs and have provided seeds, as well as such living gifts as bees, chicks, goats, and heifers. One of the most heralded programs has been the Heifer Project which was envisioned and brought to fruition by a Brethren layman, Dan West. Under this program, which is now administered interdenominationally, heifers are sent to underdeveloped areas, thus affording a long term as well as an immediate food source. Of all the service and relief programs, Heifer Project has probably received the widest attention and publicity.

In 1982 the Mennonites held their 26th annual Pennsylvania Relief Sale. These sales are held in the mammoth Harrisburg Farm Show Building and feature homemade quilts, antiques, and a vast array of other items. Quilt fanciers and collectors come from many parts of the country to see and to buy.

34

As one might expect, there is ample food with chicken barbecue, chicken corn soup, and many other Pennsylvania Dutch delicacies.

On a lesser scale, the eastern Pennsylvania Brethren have also held relief sales in recent years, and each year's sale becomes more extensive. As their name suggests, the object of these sales is to raise funds for supporting those in need, such as flood, earthquake, and refugee victims.

One of the most significant services that the plain people have and are rendering is relief to disaster victims. These disasters are particularly related to such natural catastrophes as floods and earthquakes. The Mennonite and the Brethren disaster units are well-organized and can dispatch volunteers on short notice. Countless victims of disasters have expressed their admiration for the selfless spirit of service manifested by these disaster volunteers. In many cases, these tragedies occur in places where the plain people are relatively unknown. Often a person's first contact with a Mennonite, Amish, or Brethren has been in the context of "mudding out" a house after a flood or rebuilding housing after an earthquake. The Amish also have made generous and significant contributions to these projects.

In a time when religion has become big business and the emphasis is much more often on what "Christ can do for you" than what you can do for him, the quiet, dedicated service projects of the plain people are worthy of note. How often our religious service has an ax to grind and becomes a not very subtle ego-satisfying exercise. How tempting it is to use religion to manipulate others and to get them to accept and follow our theological systems and pet ideas. One of the remarkable aspects of the disaster relief programs is the lack of proselytizing. The mission of the disaster volunteers is not to convert people to the "Anabaptist vision" but to serve those who have been victims of disaster. Aid is not dependent upon the recipient's theological orientation, nor is aid calculated by how many "souls will be saved" or converts produced. The sole criterion is human need, and there runs deeply in the "plain tradition" the notion that love of God and love of neighbor are inseparable, that the final judgment may not so much be dependent upon the correctness of our theology nor yet the zeal of our "witnessing," but upon the quality of our "fruits." Among the favorite words of Jesus for the plain people have been these: "By their fruits you shall know them" (Matt. 7:20);

"For I was hungry and you gave me food, I was thirsty and you gave me drink, I was a stranger and you welcomed me, I was naked and you clothed me, I was sick and you visited me, I was in prison and you came to me . . . Truly, I say to you, as you did it to one of the least of these my brethren, you did it to me" (Matt. 25:31-46).

The relationship between service and evangelism is a perennial problem for every Christian. It must be said that the plain people have never excelled in evangelism. Traditionally, their growth was largely dependent upon their ability to keep their own within the fold. There was little if any evangelistic outreach. But even as Brethren and Mennonites have turned increasingly to the world, evangelistic success has eluded them. It may be that they have never been able to shed their sectarian stance and image. Their isolationism, clannishness, their "peculiarity," seem to persist in spite of their more recent sophisticated and bureaucratic facades. They seemingly are still more captivated by the role of the servant and the disciple than the evangelist and the proselyter. Neither have they been given to the niceties, nuances, and mystifications of academic theology. While they were prepared to "give an account of the faith that was in them," its expression was always more practical than theoretical, always more life-centered than word-centered.

To be sure, these statements are general and overdrawn, but they reflect and characterize a mood, a milieu, which has accounted for the vitality and the dynamism that has been, and still is, present among Lancaster County's plain people. The plain peoples' interpretation of the faith is partial and needs correction, as does that of every other tradition. Nevertheless, in a time when the world increasingly is becoming "too much with us," when religion is being huckstered as a success technique and being served displaces service, when the demands and the cost of discipleship are diluted by soft living and pleasurable experiences, when we are more in step with the god of war than the Prince of Peace—then we need to look again at the plain people. For as we wrestle with the relationship between Christ and culture, as we make our pilgrimage from the "city of man" to the "city of God," their vision can be for us as light and salt and leaven.

2

The Pilgrimage of Simplicity

Among the Christian virtues which characterize the so-called plain people are nonresistance, service, community, and simplicity. Simplicity or the simple life is closely related to such qualities as humility, sincerity, and integrity. It is opposed to pride, worldliness, materialism, and complexity. Moreover, the plain people have tended to identify the simple life with the rural environment. Rural life and values have always been more congenial to simplicity than the cosmopolitanism and complexity of urban life. The farm rather than the high rise, and the plow rather than the desk, have been more in keeping with the plain people's understanding of simplicity. This pre-occupation with ruralism is perhaps the major reason why the groups which have been identified with the Anabaptist tradition have never been very successful in founding and propagating viable urban congregations. To this day the strongest Mennonite and Brethren churches are concentrated in rural and small town settings.

The simple life has also been marked by a conservative temperament. It has been nurtured in an environment marked by traditionalism and opposition to change—maintaining the status quo. As their name implies, the plain people have attempted to manifest simplicity through their manner of address and communication, informal forms of worship, meetinghouses devoid of elaborate furnishings and symbolism, houses and furniture which are functional but not ostentatious, and distinctive "plain clothes."

Simplicity has always been closely identified with nonconformity, and it is difficult to distinguish between them. The radical distinction which the plain people make between the church and the world is the basis for nonconformity. Christians are called out of the world to be a separate people. They are not to be conformed to the world nor to be "unequally yoked with unbelievers." The values of the world are in opposition to those of the Kingdom. Worldliness, with its attendant pride, power, materialism, and hedonism, is a demonic force against which the "set-apart" Christian must wage a life-long struggle. The way to the Kingdom—the way of true discipleship—is narrow and hard and "few there be that find it." On the contrary, the way of the world—the way to destruction—is broad and easy and "many there be that take it."

For the plain people, there is perhaps no more blatant expression of worldliness than that of pride, of pretentious display, or boastful showiness. In the Amish and the Old Order Mennonite congregations where the preaching is still in Pennsylvania Dutch, the term *Hochmut* recurs again and again. *Hochmut* is the essence of worldliness. It is pride, display, showiness. It is a rebellion against, or a rejection of, tradition and proper order. Opposed to *Hochmut* is *Demut*—humility, lowliness, obedience, service. This is the virtue most prized and is the one which characterizes every true citizen of the Kingdom. The Christian life is lived out in this constant tension and struggle between Christ and culture, church and world, *Demut* and *Hochmut*.

Emphasis on the simple life runs deeply in the Anabaptist-Pietist tradition. Its basic ground is not in the perpetuation of traditions and forms but in Scripture. These sectarians were "people of the Book" who believed that the Reformers had not gone far enough in their understanding of the priesthood of each believer and of Scripture alone as the basis for faith and practice. The Reformers had only gone "halfway" and had continued such practices as infant baptism, formal worship, and a too close relationship between church and state. Moreover, they tended to give priority to doctrine and theologizing rather than to ethics and the demands and cost of discipleship.

In the New Testament and especially in the Sermon on the Mount these "left-wing" reformers discerned a way of life which they believed the Reformers had neglected. There they read about nonresistance, nonswearing, and about a quality of life marked by singleness of purpose and simplicity. These virtues they took literally and they attempted to live according to Jesus' directives. But simplicity has another foundation—the lifestyle of Jesus. Jesus, they believed, lived a simple and austere life. His parents were among the "lowly" rather than the "high and mighty." His birth was in simple surroundings, traditionally thought to be a stable. He grew up in Nazareth where his father was a carpenter. When he began his Galilean ministry, Jesus called simple, unlettered, unsophisticated men to be his disciples. As far as we can discern he lived a very simple life, ate simple food and ministered to the "ordinary" people who came in multitudes to see and hear him. His simple lifestyle was underscored when he pointed out that "foxes have holes and birds have nests but the Son of Man has nowhere to lay his head" (Matt. 8:20). He had no wealth or property, and yet he was "rich toward God."

The note of *Nachfolge* or following after Jesus, of living according to his example, of discipleship, has been central to the plain people. Christianity was more a way of life than of correct beliefs. The ethical dimension of the faith was more prominent than the theological. Discipleship demanded an obedience, a discipline, and a style of life that ran counter to both one's natural inclinations and the values and standards of the prevailing culture. Thus, such concepts as being strangers and pilgrims in the world and being persecuted for Christ's sake were not merely ideas, but became for them real experiences. The cross of martyrdom is always a possibility for anyone who takes seriously the life and teachings of Jesus. The simple life, while it became overlaid with tradition, was nevertheless fed by the springs of biblical authority and the life and example of Jesus.

As one examines the New Testament, it becomes evident that there is in the teachings of both Jesus and Paul an emphasis upon freedom which runs counter to a religion of law. Jesus and Paul said that the law was fulfilled in the love of God and of neighbor. For them, the "law of love" was the divine imperative. To love God with heart, soul, mind, and strength, and to love the neighbor as one's self represented the highest vision of what one should be and do. Such love could not be legalized or coerced. Rather, it represented a spontaneous response to God's love and mercy and to the neighbor who shared in God's creative and redemptive activity.

In the Sermon on the Mount (Matt. 5, 6, 7), Jesus emphasizes the relationship between inward disposition and outward action. He presents us with an "impossible possibility." Killing is equated with hatred of one's "brother," and committing adultery is equated with "looking lustfully at a woman." Giving alms and praying are not to be advertised and displayed but are to be done in secret, and then "the Father will reward you." Jesus said that if one's eye is sound the whole body will be full of light, and conversely, if your eye is not sound, your whole body will be full of darkness. Furthermore, he cautioned about being anxious about the details of living such as acquiring food and clothing. Rather one should seek first the Kingdom and his righteousness.

This same theme comes out in a different way in Jesus' contrast between saying and doing. In his teaching about nonswearing, he cautioned against oaths and said that a simple "yes" or "no" is enough. "Anything more than this comes from evil." In the time of judgment, "not everyone who says, 'Lord, Lord,' shall enter the Kingdom of heaven, but he who does the will of my Father who is in heaven." And his Sermon on the Mount concludes with the parable of the Two Builders. The emphasis here is upon two types of response to his teachings — those who hear and do not, and those who hear and do. The former response is like the one who builds a house on sand while the latter is like one who builds on rock. The first is destroyed by the forces of nature while the second endures.

Thus, it becomes clear that for Jesus what one should be and do is related more to inward motive and disposition than to the keeping and following of laws and traditions. If the tree is sound, good fruit will result. If the spring is clean, good water will flow from it. The direction of one's commitment and devotion determine the quality of one's life. The "good life" comes from a commitment to the Author of the good rather than legalistically following rules and regulations that presume to prescribe the good. St. Augustine, in what appears initially as an incredible statement, said: "Love God and do as you please." Was he not saying that if one's devotion and center of value are focused upon God and his Kingdom, then our actions will reflect the love of God and neighbor? An ethic founded upon codes and laws and traditions can be a spiritless, constrictive, and enslaving experience. But one which represents our response to God's creative and redemptive action can be characterized by freedom, creativity, and joy.

The above has profound as well as very complex implications for an understanding and practice of simplicity. At its best, the simple life should grow out of singleminded devotion to the Kingdom. Simplicity should not be coerced nor result from our scrupulous following of orders and traditions. Rather it should be a free and devoted response to God and to the neighbor.

Today there is a renewed interest in adopting the simple life. Whereas in the past simplicity was largely viewed as a religious virture and one practiced by certain quaint religious sects or by persons holding unconventional philosophical views, now it is seen as a prudent and practical alternative. We have entered a new era threatened with scarcity rather than abundance. Moreover, our vaunted technology is demanding from us a heavy price in terms of pollution of air and water. We have been a very prodigal and wasteful people. Our consumer economy with its relentless and cunning advertising has led us to lust after a multitudinous array of things, or even junk, which we could easily live without. The ecological implications of our profligacy are evident on every hand.

We often speak of nature as our mother. "Mother nature" is a well-known and widely used term. But perhaps we should think of nature more as our sister than our mother. We, together with the natural order, are God's creation. In the Genesis account, God created humankind after he had finished the creation of what we know as nature. Nature is our sister creation and owes its existence and sustenance to God just as we do. After God had created human beings in his image and likeness, he said that they should have dominion over the fish of the sea, and over every thing that creeps upon the earth (Gen. 1:30).

The relationship between religion and nature is a complex and variegated one. As Christianity developed, it moved westward into Europe and finally to the Western Hemisphere. In the West, the industrial revolution and the capitalistic system also developed. These movements led to the domination and the exploitation of nature. Industrialism and technology required more and more natural resources to satisfy their burgeoning demands. And capitalism with its emphasis upon production and profits tended to give these priority rather than ecological considerations. The relationships between Christianity and capitalism and between Protestantism (especially Calvinism) and the work ethic are intriguing and have been explored by Weber, Tawney, and others. In our era, we are reaping the bitter harvest of our blatant rape and prostitution of our sister, nature. We in the West have exercised dominion over nature with a vengeance, and nature appears to be repaying us in kind. Many observers would say that Christianity with its "doctrine" of dominion over nature has to a large extent been responsible for our current plight. It is often

41

pointed out that in the East the juxtaposition between religion and nature is less sharp and more harmonious than it is in the West. If there is any credence to such observations, it confronts us in the "Christian West" with serious and far-reaching ethical and theological implications.

A simplicity which is grounded in a biblical perspective takes the concept of stewardship seriously. Stewardship implies that we are not the dominators of nature nor its possessors. What we have has been given to us and we are responsible not alone to ourselves, but to God and the neighbor as to how we use it. For American Christians, the problems revolving around property and wealth are among the most crucial ethical issues we confront. If we are at all morally sensitive, we cannot rest easily in our luxury and comfort while most of the world's people languish in poverty and misery. We are part of a minority of those who have much in the midst of a majority of those who have little.

Jesus had more to say about wealth and luxury than we like to think. Some of his most pointed eschatological sayings and parables have to do with wealth and poverty. The searing fires of judgment are reserved for those who bask in luxury and comfort and are insensitive to the needy neighbor. Wealth usually brings with it privilege and power, but from an ethical perspective it also brings responsibility. "For to whom much is given, of him shall much be required" (Luke 12:48). The concept of stewardship relates to the totality of our existence, to all that we are and have. But for those of us who are affluent, it impinges hard upon our wealth and our possessions.

In his Sermon on the Mount, Jesus illumined another dimension of simplicity. He cautioned against anxiety about our lives, about what we shall eat, or drink, or wear. His remedy for anxiety was to seek first God's Kingdom and his righteousness, and all these things shall be yours as well. In an age when increasingly we are becoming anxious about our national security, our economic security, our ecological security, these words of Jesus appear to be an impossible ideal. Our lives can become so cluttered by complexity and the details of living that we become enslaved to ourselves and lose a sense of perspective. Simplicity implies that there is a way "beyond the rat race," as Art Gish puts it in a recent book. To live simply is to have a center of value and a sense of priority and perspective. To focus one's attention on God's Kingdom and his righteousness is to view our lives in a wider and deeper dimension so that we perceive that the universe does not revolve around our little worlds. Rather, our lives, together with the whole universe, are sustained and ordered by God. To view life in this perspective and to entrust one's entire being to God's providence and government is to take a leap of faith. The pilgrimage of simplicity does not see the end from the beginning, but it is characterized by trust and an ultimate hope. It is described so poignantly in Hebrews 11: "By faith Abraham obeyed when he was called to go out to a place which he was to receive as an inheritance; and he went out, not knowing where he was to go. By faith he sojourned in the land of promise, as in a foreign land, living in tents with Isaac and Jacob, heirs with him of the same promise. For he looked forward to the city which has foundations, whose builder and maker is God."

The simple life, which was once a Christian virture emphasized particularly by the plain people, now is becoming more of a prudent and practical alternative for all of us. Most prognostications about the future suggest that we must simplify our lifestyle, given the limitation of the earth's resources and the continuing growth of the population. We must live simply so that others may simply live. That is the stark reality that confronts us. And so today there is a renewed interest in the convictions and practices of such groups as the Amish, the Hutterites, and the Old Order Mennonites, not for theological, but for ecological reasons. The Amish with their horse-drawn vehicles and farming equipment, their windmills, their simple clothes and household furnishings are following a lifestyle which causes a minimal amount of environmental pollution and damage.

The Aaron Zook exhibit at the People's Place (see page 27) is accompanied by an audio interpretation, and at the end a rather penetrating and self-searching question is asked. The announcer points out that the Amish are not evangelistic and do not seek outside adherents. However, the visitors are asked whether they ever considered the implications of becoming a member of the Amish community. The presentation concludes with two questions: What would you give up? and, What would you gain?

As with most areas of Christian theology and ethics, the concept or the ideal of simplicity is one thing while its implementation and practice are quite another. As noted above, the simple life should be the outward expression of an inward grace. It should represent a free, creative, and spontaneous responsiveness to our vision of the Kingdom. It should be rooted in our understanding of discipleship and should reflect our love and devotion to God and our concern for, and loyalty to, the neighbor. It should be an outgrowth of the presence of the gospel within us and among us and should not be coerced or legalized.

But for the plain people, the simple life has never been quite this "simple." There is perhaps no other area that has become so subject to laws, rules, and order, as that of simplicity. It has confronted the plain people with a complex and intricate system which attempts to spell out in detail what it means to live a life of simplicity and nonconformity. It is for this reason that the groups which come out of the Anabaptist tradition have experienced perhaps more fragmentation than any other Christian group. Among the Mennonites there have been hardly any schisms because of theological doctrines. Almost without exception the divisions have resulted from questions on discipline, particularly in relation to nonconformity. All too often nonconformity became equated with uniformity, so that any deviation from the norm resulted either in exclusion from the community or else redefining the order and starting a new movement. In their attempt to remain "pure" and "unspotted from the world," the plain people attempted the impossible task of legislating simplicity and nonconformity. It is the problem of trying to relate the changeless gospel to a changing society. The line of demarcation between the church and the world is elusive and increasingly hard to define. What often happens in a legal approach to religion is that laws and orders which are culturally and historically conditioned are invested with ultimate authority and divine sanction. This can lead to internal tension which in turn can result in schism and estrangement between groups or between generations. In order to arrest this process, the bishops and/or elders are tempted to exercise increasingly repressive and authoritarian measures, but this merely compounds the problem.

To outside observers the plethora of rules among the plain people has brought charges of inconsistency and hypocrisy. Questions like the following are thought if not expressed: Why are the Amish buggies in Lancaster County gray while those of the Old Order Mennonites are black? Why do Amish married men wear beards while Mennonites are generally clean shaven? Why do Old Order Mennonites prohibit automobiles but allow tractors for farm work? Why must their tractors be on steel instead of rubber? Why are rubber tires prohibited on tractors but allowed on bicycles? Why do Hornung Mennonites allow cars but require the chromium to be painted black? Why do Old Order Amish meet in houses instead of churches for worship? Why do Old Order Mennonites reject the use of a pulpit for a table in their churches? And what about attire? Why hooks and eyes instead of buttons? Should women wear white or black strings on their prayer coverings? Must one wear a plain suit? Or is it permissible to wear a tie, provided it is a black bow, and is worn with a plain suit? These are some of the issues which have resulted in schism, but all of which attempt to define the boundaries of simplicity and nonconformity.

It can be said that the propagation and maintenance of the idea and practice of nonconformity have been largely the result of three forces: tradition, indoctrination, and discipline. Traditions evolve, become accepted, and are invested with authority. Through practice, teaching, and preaching, indoctrination takes place. And then the community with its strong sense of identity exercises a powerful psychological discipline upon its members. If a member transgresses the order, he can be banned. For the Old Order Amish this means that the transgressor becomes an "outsider" even to his or her own family to the extent that he or she cannot eat at the family table.

But it is not simply tradition, indoctrination, and discipline which perpetuates the community. The *Ordnung* (order) arises from an attempt to be obedient to Scripture and to follow after Jesus. The difficulty is that the New Testament does not spell out in as precise detail as the plain people do the "rules" for Christian discipleship. And given the christological "bias" of the gospel writers, our knowledge about the details of the lifestyle of the historical Jesus are very meager. There are basic attitudes expressed in the New Testament concerning worldliness, purity, humility, and simplicity, but few specific directives. Paul instructs the Corinthians that women should wear long hair and that they should be veiled. In I Timothy and I Peter the writers encourage modest adornment and the rejection of gold or pearls. I remember that after I was licensed to the ministry my grandmother questioned the propriety of my wearing gold-framed glasses. Thus, from a literal reading of the New Testament and their understanding of what it means to follow after Jesus, the plain people have established standards of simplicity and noncomformity which have at times led to schism. But their basic concern was to be obedient to their vision of the Kingdom and to manifest in their lives the fact that Christian discipleship is costly because Christ and culture are never easily and harmoniously reconciled.

While charges of legalism and inconsistency can be brought against the plain people, nevertheless, they are bearing witness and pointing to a vital area of Christian ethics. The standards of a secular culture and those of the Christian community often are opposed to each other. Simplicity is a necessary antidote, both within and outside the church, to pride, self-indulgence, luxury, waste, and extravagance. H. Richard Niebuhr in his ethics classes at Yale drew the distinction between property for use and property for display. Property and possessions are a part of God's providence and as such can be rightfully used and enjoyed. But there is a thin and elusive line between use and display. Property for display is a manifestation of human pride and self-aggrandizement. It impedes rather than enhances human community and solidarity. It tempts one to define the human person by what one possesses rather than by what one is. Property used for display potentially can become idolatrous because we assign infinite worth and value to that which is finite.

On a number of occasions I have worshipped in Old Order Mennonite churches. For an outsider this is to experience another world, one which is pre-industrial and even pre-Renaissance. I have come away from these experiences with a number of impressions. For one, this community seems to have a distinct identity and knows what it is and from whence it came. There is in the community a uniformity which is paradoxically stifling and refreshing. There appears to be a studious preoccupation with order, but a noteworthy freedom from enslavement to contemporary fads, fashions, and consumerism. Social and economic distinctions are virtually non-existent because all the buggies look the same—no gradation from Fords to Cadillacs! Likewise, the clothing is uniform, so that one cannot distinguish rich from poor by the quality of the attire. The division between clergy and laity is not in evidence. Both look the same, and both represent the same educational attainment because the clergy are chosen by lot from the congregation. In addition to their ministerial responsibilities, they earn their livelihood usually by farming, the same as the majority of the congregation. Moreover, there is no raised platform or pulpit in the meetinghouse. The minister is "on the same level" as the congregation. While there is no traditional Christian symbolism in the meetinghouse and its decor is simple and even austere, this simplicity and austerity conveys its own message with unusual force and power.

Up to this point the Amish and the Old Order Mennonites have resisted, to a remarkable degree, the technological innovations and the values of a secular culture. Theirs is a much-needed witness because it serves to remind us that we are ever in danger of losing sight of the tension between church and world. In the process of acculturation and urbanization most of us who have come out of the plain people's tradition have laid aside the outward signs of our "plainness" such as plain suits and prayer coverings. But there is an issue which continues to haunt us and is not easily put to rest. How can we maintain and perpetuate the values which the visible forms embodied? And what if, after laying aside the forms, we lose sight of, and become insensitive to, the realities to which they pointed? These are relevant and vital questions for every Christian.

3

Blessed Are the Peacemakers

There are perhaps no ethical issues which have been characterized by more intense feeling and perplexity than those of the Christian and war and the relationship between church and state. Among the darkest moments in church history have been those when Christians have resorted to indescribable acts of violence and distruction, all under the aegis of the cross and the cause of the "Prince of Peace." How often has the church condoned war and even sanctified it as a "holy" crusade? It has been pointed out correctly that there is no fanaticism so intense as religious fanaticism. Moreover, it appeals to ultimate values and standards of judgment which are believed to transcend all human values and judgments. It must be said to our shame that the most warlike and bloodthirsty area of the world has been the Christian West. Our western history is replete with wars and rumors of war. And in many cases Christians on both sides of the conflict have adopted the stance of the crusader and the "happy warrior." But in recent times the mood has become more somber. After Vietnam, and in view of the ever-threatening nuclear holocaust, the mood is more and more that of the "mournful warrior."

Roland Bainton, the well-known Yale church historian, finds three positions that the church has taken historically in relation to war: pacifism, just war, and the crusade. The first position, that of pacifism, was the prevailing view from the time of Christ to Constantine. During this early period the Christians were a persecuted group who stood on the periphery of the policies and activities of the Roman Empire. From the end of the New Testament period down to 170-80 A.D. there is no evidence of Christians in the army.

With the conversion to Christianity of the emperor Constantine in the early part of the fourth century, changes took place in the life of the church. The nature of these changes and the reasons for them have been a persistent topic of debate among church historians. One school of thought sees this time as the corruption of Christianity or its "fall," as G. J. Heering terms it. The church, which had been a persecuted minority was now accepted by the Empire. The church became a respectable institution and increasingly the cleavage between the church and the Empire was ameliorated. The Christians became more acculturated and adopted the patterns and ideals of a cosmopolitan culture. Service in the army became more acceptable. Thus, for Heering and others Christianity fell and lost its former genius, especially in regard to its pacifist witness.

At the other pole of this debate are those who do not see any radical change in the church with the conversion of Constantine, but rather point to a continuing trend which had been in process long before his time. Umphrey Lee believes that the conversion of Constantine was not the occasion of any sudden capitulation of the church. The growing conformity to the world resulted from the spread of the gospel throughout the Mediterranean world. With the increase of numbers there were also more people who shrank from the harsher demands of the gospel and were satisfied with an approximation to the faith.

However the period of Constantine is to be interpreted, the fact remains that after his time a different emphasis was introduced in relation to the church and war. The enthusiasm accompanying the cessation of persecution apparently diverted the leaders of the church from immediately considering the ethical problems involved in military service. It remained for St. Augustine to formulate a new approach which has had far-reaching influence in both Roman Catholic and Protestant Christianity.

The period from Constantine to the barbarian invasions of the Empire witnessed the emergence of the just war idea. Augustine, appealing to Platonic and Stoic motifs, formulated what has subsequently been called the theory of the just war. This theory embodied three criteria for the waging of a just war. The first condition was that the *object* of the war must be just, namely, to vindicate justice and to restore peace. Secondly, the *conduct* of the war must be just, observing good faith and humanity, avoiding treachery, wanton violence and injury to noncombatants. To these two classical requirements Augustine added a third—the just *intention*, which is to benefit alike the victim and the oppressor by protection for the one and a benevolent restraint of the other. Thus, although participation in a just war is morally right, a sensitive and sinful person will not rejoice in the task of discipline; rather war will be waged with a heavy heart and with a mournful spirit. This ethic of the just war as developed by Augustine has had a strong influence, especially in Roman Catholicism, but also in many branches of Protestantism to the present time.

The Middle Ages introduced a third position in regard to the church and war—the crusade. The first of eight crusades against the Moslems in the Holy Land was encouraged by Pope Urban II in 1095. The crusades were marked by decreasing restraint and increasing passion and enthusiasm. The clergy themselves in many instances took an active part in the crusades which were in effect "holy wars" thought to be sanctioned by God and even commanded by him. The crusaders were led into battle behind the cross of Jesus Christ. These encounters were in defense of the true faith and for the purpose of delivering the Holy Land from the enemies of God and Christ.

These three positions—pacifism, the just war, and the crusade—with varying emphases have been held by Christians throughout the history of the church. Catholicism subscribes to the theory of the just war. The groups emerging from the Protestant Reformation can be grouped roughly as follows: the Lutherans and Anglicans adopted the just war, the Calvinists endorsed the crusade, and left-wing groups such as Mennonites and Quakers were pacifist.

The mood of the churches in reference to war has tended to change from time to time depending upon the causes and goals of a given war. The mass media and the use of propaganda have also had influential bearing upon the fervor and commitment with which a war was waged.

During the First World War all except resolute pacifists swung to the crusading position. Many pulpits in the Christian church were used as recruiting stations and for the purpose of selling liberty bonds. Some ministers used their pulpits to defend the "righteous war" through appeal to Scripture and even the authority of Jesus Christ himself. It was a time, as the title of one book had it, when "preachers presented arms." This was the war to end all wars and the one that would make the world safe for democracy.

Following World War I, the American churches engaged in

a widespread peace crusade and official statements from practically all the churches denounced war and affirmed that they would never again support war. But with the outbreak of the Second World War this pacifist enthusiasm receded, and Christians who took the pacifist position were only a small minority.

With the coming of World War II, the high hopes and idealism attending World War I were frustrated and shattered. Now the mood was more restrained, and with few exceptions the crusading spirit gave way to the mournful spirit. This time pulpits were not used to present arms. There was a task to be accomplished from which the glory and adventure had been sapped by the grim realization that military might and war would not lead us to the "promised land." And with the dawn of the atomic age in August 1945 the mournful mood became even more pronounced, because now there was a means of destruction so awesome that the future of civilization hung in the balance.

This situation caused many Christians to regard themselves as "nuclear pacifists." With the advent of nuclear weapons and their potential for incalculable and unimaginable destruction, the criteria for the waging of a just war became irrelevant and meaningless. The very thought of a nuclear holocaust is so terrible that war itself is no longer the lesser of two evils but the *worst* conceivable evil. Consequently, the nuclear pacifist cannot participate in war because we have crossed a threshold where modern nuclear warfare is not simply a difference in degree insofar as past wars are concerned, but is a difference in kind. For the nuclear pacifist there is nothing more demonic than a war waged with nuclear weapons, and therefore participation in such warfare must be categorically rejected.

With the coming of the 1960s and the United States' involvement in the Vietnam debacle, the anti-war movement became more passionate and widespread than at any time in American history. Many young men of draft age fled to Canada, Sweden, and other nations to escape the draft. Desertion from the armed forces became a serious problem. Large scale demonstrations and acts of civil disobedience became commonplace on college campuses, at military installations, and in our nation's capital. As many as 50,000 Americans lost their lives in Vietnam in a cause which was perhaps the most divisive that the American people have ever experienced. The mood which attended the Vietnam conflict was not so much

52

mournful as it was one of hostility and open rebellion. It became apparent that our nation had overextended its capabilities. The world had changed radically since World War II and we could no longer police the world and work our will as we once could. The rising tides of nationalism and movements toward liberation in the Third World introduced new dimensions in international relations and exercised restraints upon us that we had not known previously.

After Vietnam and the arrival of the 1970s, it became apparent that much of the anti-war sentiment was directed against the Vietnam War and not against war in general. The radicalism of the 1960s gave way to a quietism that marked the 1970s. This was the decade which witnessed a growing Russian challenge to our economic and military supremacy. Now one hears talk again about "military action" on our part, of just wars, and of limited nuclear wars. It is evident that the 1980s are marked by serious problems for us and for the entire world. The arms race continues to plague us and diverts and wastes resources which are desperately needed for constructive purposes. There is ample evidence that it fuels the inflation which threatens the world economy. We live in a very dangerous world where nuclear arms are proliferating and where more nations will develop them. While our world is confronted with very serious and seemingly insurmountable problems, none is more urgent than the prevention of war with its potential for total annihilation.

Any discussion about the Christian and war and the relationship between church and state must give special attention to three groups which since their respective beginnings have continuously opposed war and worked for peace. These are the so-called historic peace churches—the Friends, the Mennonites, and the Brethren. While their numbers are relatively small in comparison with many other Christian bodies, their witness and their constructive and imaginative contributions have been remarkably significant and noted internationally.

While the historic peace churches share a common interest in peace and peacemaking, in preventing war and in "binding up the wounds of war," and while they have at times cooperated in these efforts, they nevertheless reflect differing theological and ethical presuppositions. These distinctions often are delineated by reference to the difference between "nonresistance" and "pacifism." Nonresistance characterizes the classical Anabaptist-Mennonite position, while pacifism is the position of the Friends. The Brethren perhaps represent a mediating position, with strong ties to nonresistance, but having now more nearly identified themselves with the pacifist stance. How shall we understand the terms "nonresistance" and "pacifism" and how shall we distinguish between them, since they are so frequently used interchangeably?

Any discussion of nonresistance and pacifism is at once involved with the question of the relationship between church and state. According to the Anabaptist-Mennonite view, the church is a fellowship, community, brotherhood — a *Gemeinde*. It is not to be conceived primarily in institutional terms although it is not without structure. There is a sharp distinction between church and world, between Christ and culture. The Christian way sets one apart from the world because discipleship implies nonconformity and obedience to Jesus Christ. There are two worlds or two kingdoms, and while they are related, the disciple of Christ is called upon to "seek first the Kingdom of God." Here is the authentic Christian's center of value and devotion.

These motifs were grounded in the Anabaptist view of the authority of the Scriptures, especially the New Testament, and more particularly the Sermon on the Mount. The Sermon on the Mount was a manifesto for citizens of the Kingdom. It portrayed the style of life which was necessary if one would follow Jesus and be his disciple. It was the word, intent, and spirit of Jesus which was the guiding principle of biblical interpretation. Not the word itself, but the Word which became flesh was the ultimate norm for faith and practice.

How then did this "vision" apply to the relationship between church and state? Any notion of a church-state union or *corpus Christianum* was categorically rejected. The Anabaptist view is a sharp dualism between church and state. The true church is a set-apart, redeemed community. It consists of those voluntary believers who have been called out of the kingdom of darkness into the kingdom of light. Thus, the realm of the state must function "outside the perfection of Christ." But the Anabaptists are not anarchists. Government is ordained by God and is necessary to preserve order and to punish evildoers. Thus, in keeping with the Reformers, the Anabaptists viewed the state as an expression of both the wrath and the grace of God. Government, therefore, has its rightful place and its decrees should be obeyed and respected insofar as "temporal" affairs are concerned. The New Testament enjoins us to pray

54

for those in authority and to pay taxes. But the state's power is never absolute. It functions under the sovereignty of God. The state oversteps its powers if and when it infringes upon the realm of faith or the realm of Christ. When this happens the state may be rightfully disobeyed.

A very real example of the continuing tension the issue of the separation of church and state raises might be seen in a change that has taken place in the Akron (Pa.) Church of the Brethren. The old Akron church sanctuary, which was the congregation's meetinghouse during my youth, reflected the Pennsylvania Dutch penchant for orderliness and upkeep and was plain with minimal symbolism. In recent years, that building has been replaced by an imposing new structure, the exterior and interior of which are aesthetically pleasing and attractive. Upon entering the new sanctuary a large suspended cross captures the worshiper's attention.

But a significant innovation in the new church is the addition of the American and the Christian flags to the chancel area. I confess that my sectarian background causes me problems here. As for the Christian flag, I never recall having heard about its history and symbolism. There seems to be a notable dearth of material and teaching about its meaning and significance. I tend to conclude that it accompanies the national flag in churches in order to make the latter more palatable. The presence of the national flag in a church symbolizes for me that which runs counter to the stance of the radical reformers of the sixteenth century. The close alliance and even union between church and state was one of their major concerns. The free, believers' church which they envisioned was one in which there was separation between church and state. Their rejection of infant baptism and their insistence upon "believers' baptism" proclaimed that national citizenship and church membership are not synonomous or coterminous. To "follow after Christ" and to be a disciple is always to experience a radical tension between Christ and culture, church and world, and church and state.

The national flag in a church points toward a "culture religion" and toward a view of the church's relation to the world and to the state which is at variance with the tradition which owes its heritage to the Anabaptist wing of the Reformation. It appears to me that there is a basic contradiction in the symbolism implied by linking the cross and the national flag. The flag symbolizes exclusiveness and a particular national

55

entity and culture while the cross points to an inclusiveness which transcends national and geographical boundaries. The gospel is for "whosoever will," and in Christ there is neither "Jew nor Greek, slave nor free" (Gal. 3:28), but we are all one in him. The flag symbolizes for me an exclusiveness characterized by national pride and identity. The cross on the other hand should make us aware of sin—individual, corporate, and national. It should point us not to pride, power, or wealth, but to humility and service, and to confession and repentance for doing what we should not have done and leaving undone what we should have done.

As American Christians we are burdened with responsibility and with guilt because of our power and wealth. We above any other people are those to whom much has been given and consequently from whom much will be required. We are a privileged, wealthy, and powerful nation, and while we like to sing that "God shed his grace on thee," we need constantly to be reminded that God's judgment also rests upon us. The cross points to the cost of discipleship, to the cleavage between Christ and culture, between church and state, to our need for repentance and for salvation, and to our willingness to serve rather than to be served. But the symbolism of the national flag together with the cross is confusing because they point in different directions and present images which are not readily reconcilable.

Respect and gratitude for our national heritage is a basic dimension of our existence. We were born and nurtured in a given culture with its history, its values, its ideals, and its hopes. These are a vital part of each one of us. But if they become our god and our highest center of value, then we are guilty of idolatry, because we have put a lesser god above the true God. It is right and proper to display the flag on and in government and public buildings, parks, and post offices, and around our homes if we choose to do so. But because of the above reasons, I am not convinced that displaying the flag in the church is appropriate.

As for the Christian's participation in government, since the principles underlying the office of government are of a forceful and coercive nature, the true Christian cannot hold a government office. In this matter of governmental participation there was a distinct difference between the Anabaptists and the Reformers. Luther set forth the doctrine of the two kingdoms. In his teaching about nonresistance, Christ is not tampering with the responsibility and authority of the government, but he is teaching individual Christians how to live personally, apart from their official position and authority. Luther distinguishes between the person and the office, for these two are present simultaneously in the same person. A Christian may carry on all sorts of secular business with impunity — not as a Christian but as a secular person — while his heart remains pure in his Christianity, as Christ demands. Luther says that Christ's word, "Do not resist evil," applies to one's personal life apart from the secular government. Thus when a Christian goes to war or when he sits on a judge's bench punishing his neighbor, or when he registers an official complaint, he is not doing this as a Christian but as a soldier or a judge or a lawyer. At the same time he keeps a Christian heart. He does not intend anyone any harm, and it grieves him that his neighbor must suffer grief. So he lives simultaneously as a Christian toward everyone, personally suffering all sorts of things in the world, and as a secular person, maintaining, using, and performing all the functions required by the civil and domestic laws of his territory or city. This distinction enables a Christian not to resist any evil, but within the limits of his secular office he should oppose every evil. The resistance to evil, the administration of justice, and punishment should be left to the one who holds a position in the secular realm. As for the disciples of Christ, they should try to follow his commands.

The Anabaptists with their emphasis on following Jesus and their literal reading of the Scriptures could not accept Luther's views. According to Hans J. Hillerbrand in his doctoral dissertation on the political ethics of the Anabaptists, they rejected participation in government for four basic reasons: (1) The example of Christ himself speaks against it; (2) There is in the Scriptures no evidence for such participation by a true Christian; (3) The teachings of Christ show an incompatibility between the worldly principles of lordship and might in government rule and the suffering-servant posture of the Christian; (4) A radical church-world distinction means the Christian is solely concerned with following Christ and does not have responsibilities for maintaining law and order in the world.

The Anabaptist position takes literally Christ's admonition not to resist evil. Nonresistance is an absolute which must govern the Christian in his relationship to others and in his relationship to the state. And since the state is involved with power and the capacity and necessity to resist, the Christian cannot participate in its activities. The basis for this position is the command and example of Christ, and it must be the supreme ethic for the true Christian disciple.

It is at this point that the distinction between nonresistance and pacifism must be made. As we have noted, the Anabaptist position is one of nonresistance or defenselessness. The emphasis is upon suffering for Christ's sake, upon turning the other cheek, going the second mile, enduring injustice and persecution, rather than resisting and inflicting harm to anyone. Moreover, this is not a technique for building the Kingdom of God on earth or for Christianizing the social order. The Anabaptist view of the world is pessimistic; it is the realm of evil and darkness. The Christian is called to be separate from the world and to "come out from among them." Nonconformity rather than social transformation is the stance of one who would be a citizen of the Kingdom. Not "Christ the transformer of culture," but "Christ against culture," characterizes the Anabaptist way.

The stance of the pacifist is otherwise. The pacifist ideal is to devise a strategy for the reshaping of society. Culture is not evil, but it has the potentiality for renewal and rebirth. The pacifist brings the eschatological vision into the present so that peace on earth, good will to all becomes a present possibility. The kingdoms of this world can be transformed into the Kingdom of our Lord and of his Christ (Rev. 11:15). The Kingdom of God can be realized to a significant degree here and now.

The pacifist speaks not so much about nonresistance as about nonviolent resistance. The forces of evil are to be resisted, but with nonviolent means. The struggles of Ghandi against the British in India and of Martin Luther King, Jr., against racism are patterns to be adopted and techniques to be used in the continuing battles with evil and injustice. Absolute pacifists would enjoin governments to renounce force and violence and to conduct foreign policy by nonviolent means. Evil is not overcome by the exercise of more evil, but evil can only be overcome by good. In a well-known Quaker phrase, "Speak truth to power."

Pacifism is not "passivism," but is notably active. Among its strategies are lobbying government leaders and officials on issues related to peace and war, nonviolent demonstrations and marches, hunger strikes, civil disobedience, and refusal to pay "war taxes." Not quietism and defenselessness, but social action and involvement are the pacifist's strategy. Unlike the Anabaptists, the pacifists do not reject participation in government. Holding public office is particularly desirable because then one has the opportunity to influence and shape public policy and hopefully can move the power structures in the direction of pacifist objectives. One Brethren pacifist and social activist used to say that the Christian's duty and responsibility is to "get into the smoke-filled rooms and help clear the air."

Theologically, pacifism has had a close affinity with Protestant liberalism and the social gospel movement. Such motifs as the sacredness of human personality, confidence in progress and the future, the centrality and spirit of Jesus Christ, social idealism, the attempt to reconcile Christ and culture, and the Kingdom of God as a present and imminent reality have been basic presuppositions which have undergirded and motivated the pacifist witness and strategy.

Whatever the theological and practical differences between the classical Anabaptist position of nonresistance and of pacifism may be, both share a common conviction that war is sin and that Christ calls Christians to be peacemakers. Thus, the historic peace churches have been in the forefront in witnessing for peace and in developing alternatives to violence and warfare. As noted earlier, the Friends, the Mennonites, and the Brethren have been noted for their ministries of relief to victims of war and natural disasters. Through official statements, seminars, cooperative conferences, international work camps, voluntary service, refugee resettlement, and in many other ways, they have attempted to spread the gospel of peace and to witness to the Kingdom's presence in our world. They have taken literally Jesus' admonition in the parable of the Last Judgment that to feed the hungry, to give drink to the thirsty, to welcome the stranger, to clothe the naked, and to visit those in prison is to do it to Christ himself (Matt. 25:31-46).

The coming of war confronts everyone with a tragic moral dilemma, and this is especially true for members of the historic peace churches. In spite of the universal desire and prayer for peace, wars and rumors of war continue to plague us. What should be the Christian's response when war comes? As noted, the historic peace churches have held that participation in war is contrary to the will of God and the spirit of Jesus, and they

59

have consequently urged their members to be conscientious objectors.

In each of the wars in which the United States has participated, the historic peace churches have attempted to maintain their peace witness. During wartime the peace stand is usually unpopular and results in social ostracism and even persecution of those who refuse participation.

During the Revolutionary War, fines and taxes were levied for not joining "Associations" which were companies of volunteer soldiers. The Civil War witnessed the obnoxious practice of exemption from military service by getting a substitute or paying $300 to hire one. The Confederacy provided for exemption of conscientious objectors by allowing them to secure a substitute or to pay $500 into the public treasury.

With the coming of World War I more specific provision was made for conscientious objectors. The law of May 18, 1917, exempted members of peace churches from military service but added that "no person shall be exempted from service in any capacity which the President shall declare noncombatant." President Wilson finally defined noncombatant service as including only military service. Many conscientious objectors who could not accept noncombatant service were subjected to mistreatment and torture.

It was World War II that saw the most extensive provision for conscientious objectors with the establishment of the Civilian Public Service (CPS) program. Provision for Civilian Public Service was incorporated into the Selective Training and Service Act which became law on September 16, 1940. Civilian Public Service was under civilian control and was financed by the churches, particularly the historic peace churches which administered and provided directors for their various projects. Among the types of projects were soil conservation, forest service, national park service, agriculture, dairying, mental hospitals and training schools, public health, medical experimentation, and relief training and service.

Between May 1941 and March 1947, 11,996 conscientious objectors were drafted and assigned to Civilian Public Service camps where they performed "work of national importance." Of these, 4,665 or 38 percent were Mennonites, 1,353 were Brethren, 951 were Friends. A small minority rejected all conscription and went to prison. Thus, of the three historic peace churches, the Mennonites held most consistently to the peace position. They made participation in war or joining the armed forces a test of membership while the Brethren and the Friends generally left it to the "individual conscience." While a number of Mennonites joined the armed forces, the vast majority of Friends and Brethren did so. Less then ten percent of the Brethren and of the Friends entered CPS or noncombatant military service. This has raised the question as to whether the Friends and the Brethren can rightfully be called peace church-es since only a minority of their youth follow this practice. Nevertheless, through official statements and their varied "peace projects," both the Friends and the Brethren, together with the Mennonites, have continued their peace witness. At this writing there is a "New Call to Peacemaking" which is a cooperative effort of the historic peace churches to "explore the implications of our calling as peacemakers."

With the termination of Civilian Public Service and our country's subsequent engagement in wars in Korea and Viet-nam, provision for conscientious objectors continued. They were allowed to do alternate service in lieu of military service. One difference from CPS was that the conscientious objectors were now paid the prevailing wage in their respective jobs, whereas in CPS they were not paid but usually received a minimal allowance from the churches.

For some years now there has been no draft, but registra-tion has been reinstated. Many observers regard this as a pre-liminary step to the draft. What provisions will be made for conscientious objectors is unknown. It is possible that exemp-tions for them may not be as generous as in the recent past. As long as Christians take seriously the life and teachings of Jesus, there will always be those who for conscience sake can-not participate in war. Their perception of what belongs to Christ and what belongs to Caesar will cause them to be out of step with many of their contemporaries. Their vision will be one of a peaceable kingdom where "nation shall not lift up sword against another, neither shall they learn war anymore" (Isa. 2:4). Toward that end they will devote themselves with heart, soul, mind, and strength.

In any discussion of pacifism about a Christian point of view, the Bible and especially the teachings and character of Jesus are the primary norms and sources of authority. Pacifists find their position best vindicated in the life and teachings of Jesus, particularly in the Sermon on the Mount. They have consistently insisted that Jesus himself was a pacifist, and that his teachings, and more especially his style of life, lend an unwavering authority to the pacifist position. The major basis for the Anabaptist-Mennonite position of nonresistance comes from a literal reading of Jesus' words in the Sermon on the Mount. "You have heard that it was said, 'An eye for an eye and a tooth for a tooth.' But I say to you, do not resist one who is evil. But if any one strikes you on the right cheek, turn to him the other also; and if any one would sue you and take your coat, let him have your cloak as well; and if any one forces you to go one mile, go with him two miles" (Matt. 5:38-40).

But even more significant than his teachings and his sayings were his life and conduct. His personal relationships were marked by love and compassion. He never let his own selfish desires prevent him from giving attention and ministering to the one in need. The climax of this way of absolute love and self-renunciation is seen in the events which led to his crucifixion. Even though he could have escaped and could have resisted his enemies, he chose the way of nonresistance and redemptive suffering.

These motifs of love and nonresistance are not confined to the gospels but are found in other New Testament writings. Thus, we read that love bears all things, believes all things, hopes all things, and endures all things. We are told to bless those who persecute us, and to repay no one evil for evil. We are cautioned never to avenge ourselves, to feed and give drink to the enemy, and to overcome evil with good.

In the gospels and in other passages from the New Testament, there is, therefore, strong sanction for nonresistance. The love commandment which demands renunciation of the self in the interests of the neighbor is unconditional and uncompromising. The highest expression of the Christian ethic is a love which surrenders completely all selfish interests and all personal advantage in the service of God and neighbor. The cross of Christ is among other things the expression of the highest ethical possibility. It is a symbol of a love which suffers and takes upon itself the estrangement and the sins of the neighbor, whether enemy or friend. In the New Testament, then, we find a love ethic — a law of love — which is absolute in its claims and its demands. In view of this preponderant scriptural authority for nonresistance, it is a source of constant amazement that many Christians who argue fervently for biblical authority and inspiration and who claim to be "Bible-believing Christians," are nevertheless among the most chauvinistic and militaristic. While the Anabaptists took the Scriptures seriously and viewed them as the norm for faith and practice, they seemingly did not accept all Scripture as of equal authority. Their insistence upon discipleship and following Jesus led them to regard the living Word—the Word made flesh in Jesus Christ—as the ultimate norm. If every word of Scripture is equally authoritative, then the wars and brutality narrated in parts of the Old Testament are on an equal par with the Sermon on the Mount and I Corinthians 13. And it is not difficult to understand why a literalistic reading of the Bible would favor the former rather than the latter, especially in wartime with its attendant propaganda, patriotism, and fanaticism.

But there are also several instances recorded in the gospels which have been used by nonpacifists to support their views. Chief among these is Jesus' driving out the moneychangers from the temple. The Fourth Gospel says that Jesus made a whip of cords and drove them and their sheep and oxen out of the temple, poured out the coins, and overturned the tables (John 2:15). At another time Jesus said that he did not come to bring peace on earth but a sword (Matt. 10:34). And in the Upper Room, according to Luke, Jesus told the disciples to buy swords, if they had none, by selling their mantles (Luke 22:36). These passages, which have been subject to various interpretations, have been used by non-pacifists to "prove" that Jesus supported violence in certain situations. But in view of the vast majority of his sayings, and especially of the life he lived and the death he endured, there is meager justification for the claim that Jesus sanctioned violence and that we can adjust his radical love commandment to our violence, and what is more, to our modern means of warfare. If the pacifist position is vulnerable, it is not because we lift scriptural proof texts from their context, all the while ignoring the life and character of Jesus. Pacifists are right when they remind us that the gospels and the rest of the New Testament *do* support the way of nonviolence and that warmaking represents a blatant violation of our love to God and neighbor.

The crucial issue between the pacifist and the nonpacifist arises when we move from the traditional Anabaptist position of nonresistance to that of modern pacifism where nonviolence or nonviolent resistance is regarded as a strategy or technique for peace and/or social change. In an individual to individual confrontation, the way of nonresistance and unconditional love is a possibility. One can literally turn the other cheek, go the second mile, give one's cloak as well as one's coat; in a word, follow the path of nonresistance. The ideal of Christian love eschews violence and demands complete self-renunciation in the interests of the neighbor. The Sermon on the Mount confronts us with the demands of love which are absolute and unambiguous. In my relationship with the neighbor I have the freedom to choose the way of nonresistance to evil. I can accept violence against me rather than inflict it upon others. I can choose to "lay down my life" rather than to take the life of another. I have the option of taking the path of radical discipleship which entails the discipline of nonresistance, of enduring persecution, of loving friend and foe alike, of responding to the evil in another, not by an equal or superior show of evil, but conversely, by love and nonresistance.

Modern pacifism has maintained that what is a possible response between one individual and another is also possible between groups and even between nations. Thus, the radical love ethic of the Sermon on the Mount is viewed as a prudential social ethic. The love commandment is regarded as a strategy in international relations which will lead to a peaceful world. The command of absolute love is relevant to complex social relationships in the same way that one can renounce self-interest in a relationship with a neighbor. So pacifists at times have called upon their governments to take the "way of the cross," to unilaterally disarm, or to meet aggression by nonviolent resistance and civil disobedience. These are strategic and prudential alternatives to the arms race and the attempt to gain security through more and better means of destruction and defense. There is a moral and spiritual force and power in nonviolence that has the potentiality of converting and transforming the enemy. And even if the way of nonviolence should "fail" and the nation would be overrun and conquered, that response would represent our highest statesmanship. Such a strategy would show to the world that, more than any other, we are a nation under God and that in God we trust. Such a "defeat" would only be temporary because "truth crushed to earth will rise again," and because the ultimate victory belongs to those whose obedience and devotion is centered not in the kingdoms of this world but in the Kingdom of God.

While pacifists have viewed the law of love as a strategic

possibility in international relations, nonpacifists have held that what is a possibility in one to one relationships becomes an "impossible possibility" in the relationships between social groups and particularly nation-states. And the major reason for this is that nations are involved not only with the ideal of love, but also with the necessity for maintaining justice. The state is composed of diverse constituencies, of competing groups, of economic, social, and political considerations and entanglements. By its very nature, the state is involved with power and it exerts force upon its own people as well as upon other nations. The state has the obligation to maintain order and to attempt to secure justice both internally and externally. It is not a matter of renouncing power politics and the use of force, but of using them responsibly to ensure justice and domestic tranquility. To say that the individual should follow the way of love in his or her relationships with the neighbor is one thing, while to insist that the nation-state does the same is quite another. I can choose to take the way of the cross when confronted by the demands of another because my decision need not be unduly influenced by the implications of justice. But with the nation it is otherwise. The "right" or the "ideal" choices are never open to the nation. Rather the nation's choices are always between varying shades of gray rather than between black and white, and always between rough degrees of justice rather than between perfect good and total evil. And even if the nation were to take the way of nonresistance, it could not give up its life, or be a martyr in the sense that an individual can. The nation would still live on and the effects of its decisions would have a manifold bearing upon the status of international order and justice.

There is no doubt that the decisions and policies of a nation have a vital bearing upon the "Christian" stance of that nation. In every decision there is the potential for progress toward or denial of justice and thus a movement toward or away from the ideals of the Kingdom of God. But to realize peace and justice through a national strategy based on love and nonviolence is an impossibility given the condition of human sinfulness. Such a vision will be fulfilled only when the kingdoms of this world shall become the kingdom of our Lord and of his Christ. This does not imply that the Christian should abandon the world nor submit to a fatalistic resignation to the status quo. Rather, the Christian's vocation is to become involved with those forces and movements and to support those national and international decisions and policies which seek to redress injustice and to move the world, however imperceptibly, toward the ideal of a more humane and caring society.

But in spite of our best efforts and all our praying and working for a peaceful world, war and violence still persist. And when war comes, the Christian is confronted with one of the most crucial and perplexing moral dilemmas. Shall one be a conscientious objector to war or a conscientious participant in war? Given the passionate responses which wars engender, it is sometimes difficult to admit that conscience is present on both sides. There are those who because of religious training and belief must be conscientious objectors to war. For them, warfare is so contrary to their understanding of Christian discipleship and so at variance with the spirit and teachings of Jesus that they cannot engage in it. There are others who conscientiously participate in war because for them such issues as freedom and tyranny, justice and injustice, are at stake. For them resistance is a lesser evil than the social, economic, and political upheavals which may result from their refusal to resist. Their hope is that some semblance of order and justice may be wrested, even from the hell of war, upon which new possibilities for peace and peacemaking may be founded. The nuclear pacifist would point out that given the destructive potential of modern warfare, such possibilities no longer exist.

Some pacifists contend that to take the way of the cross will achieve the same result as war is intended to achieve, namely political success. But the way of the cross as taken by Jesus Christ, the way of friendship and martyrdom, will in all probability not lead to political success but to crucifixion. And while the absolute pacifist may be morally and spiritually ready for such an ordeal, the vast majority of others are not. Can one urge them to accept a commitment and to take a course of action for which they are not spiritually prepared?

After war comes we can often look back and say that if this or that decision had been different, the situation might be otherwise and war might have been averted. But by virtue of my citizenship and my being part of this country and its people, it is well-nigh impossible to will not to share the guilt and the consequences of our wrong decisions which finally lead to war. I accept the benefits of this country and have consented in this kind of government. I am part of this nation and this people and share in their sin. But when war comes, the pacifist is saying in essence that he can go so far with his fellow citizens but no farther. There is a rupturing of the bonds of national community and social solidarity because the pacifist seeks to be responsible to an ultimate vision of peace and goodwill which is negated by warfare. There is a "cross" and a "pain" in this decision which troubles the sensitive conscience. When those who wield power and engage in statecraft participate in war the absolute ideal of love becomes an impossibility. And for every Christian participant in war, war serves as a judgment upon our sin and our inability and unwillingness to seek first the Kingdom. For conscientious objectors there is judgment also because our decision not to participate in warfare is to a great degree a choice between purity and responsibility, between moral perfection and the struggle for justice. It is separating oneself from the neighbor in the sense that while the goal of peace is the objective of both conscientious objector and conscientious participant, nevertheless, the "means of our warfare" lead us in different directions and of necessity temporarily separate us one from the other.

The ethical implications of war and peace have occupied most of us during our entire lives. We participated in world wars in 1917 and during the 1940s. After that came the Korean War and the Vietnamese conflict. And now it appears that many of our young people will be called to decide once again whether they will be conscientious objectors or conscientious participants. Such choices are agonizing because they must be decided in the depths of our being. They are truly choices of conscience because they involve our commitment to faith and our vision of what it means to be responsible persons.

Few Christians would deny that there is a radical inconsistency between the life and teachings of Jesus and warfare, and that Jesus advocated nonresistance to evil. Christians differ as to whether nonresistance, nonviolence, or nonviolent resistance can be implemented into political and social strategies or possible alternatives in international relations. But there will and must always be those whose vocation it is to witness to the radical demands of love even though these demands may not be a practical possibility during wartime. There is need for the dissenter whose reading of the Scriptures and whose religious training and belief keep before the entire Christian community the realization that war is sin and the result of sin, that military might itself is never ultimate and that it can never be the final remedy for the evils which beset our world. Those who are called to the way of nonresistance see it as a vital dimension of Christian discipleship. Their witness will continue to remind all of us that war is a blatant denial of all that Christ taught and lived, that conscience is a part of the image of God which we bear and that it can never be coerced, and that there is a moral peril in the increasing power of the state. To this vocation of nonresistance, members of the peace churches especially will continue to respond because they have been nurtured in a tradition which emphasizes peace and peacemaking as integral parts of the Christian faith and life. Without their witness, and that of others like them, the church of Christ would be the poorer. Their vocation has been to keep before us the ideals of love and service and peace and reconciliation in peacetime as well as in wartime. They have attempted to be obedient and to follow the way of him who said that the peacemakers are blessed for they shall be called sons and daughters of God.

In a capsule statement on the nature, the meaning, and the implications of the Incarnation, Paul said that God through Christ reconciled us to himself and has given to us the ministry or reconciliation (2 Cor. 5:18). To that vocation of peacemaking and reconciliation Christians will continue to be called as long as they take seriously the demands of Christ and his gospel.

4

Members One of Another

In his well-known essay, "The Anabaptist Vision," Harold S. Bender suggested that this vision consisted of three basic elements: (1) The essence of Christianity as discipleship, (2) A new conception of the church as a brotherhood, and (3) A new ethic of love and nonresistance. It is with the second of these that we are concerned in this chapter.

One of the fundamental marks of the church according to the Anabaptist view is that it is a brotherhood, or perhaps better, a community—a *Gemeinde*. In their rejection of infant baptism the so-called left-wing reformers insisted that baptism should be reserved for those who make a free and voluntary decision to follow Christ and to become members of the Christian community. This view moved away from the traditional pattern of the close relationship between church and state toward one where church and state were separate. In medieval and post-Reformation Europe, citizenship and church membership were practically coterminous. For the radical reformers discipleship was costly; as Jesus suggested, one must "count the cost" before deciding whether or not to become a Christian (Luke 14:28). To be a Christian was not a matter of birth, but of rebirth, as it were. The *Gemeinde* was a free and voluntary association of those who had counted the cost and who subsequently chose the way of discipleship. The cost for many of the early radical reformers was martyrdom because they had taken a position and expounded beliefs which were counter to the powerful and pervasive church-state establishment. This cleavage between sect and church (to use Troeltsch's typology) is evidenced by the differing understandings of the nature of the church and of the Christian life as symbolized by infant and believers' baptism. The church type is marked by inclusiveness and universality. Its ideal is that the church should embrace culture and even dominate it and transform it. The sect type, on the other hand, is exclusive. It is composed of those who have been called out of the world into a new community whose beliefs and lifestyle are at variance with those of the world. Culture is not to be welcomed and embraced; rather, it is to be rejected because it is an enemy and a threat to those who earnestly seek to follow Christ.

The concept of the church as a community or a *koinonia* (fellowship) did not originate with the Anabaptists. This view is rooted in the New Testament and was dramatically exemplified in the life and practices of the primitive Christian church. The book of Acts describes the original community, immediately after Pentecost, as follows: "And all who believed were together and had all things in common; and they sold their possessions and goods and distributed them to all, as any had need. And day by day, attending the temple together and breaking bread in their homes, they partook of food with glad and generous hearts, praising God and having favor with all the people. And the Lord added to their number day by day those who were being saved" (Acts 2:44-47). It was this pattern, this vision of the church, that the Anabaptists tried to follow. They attempted to go back beyond the medieval church, and even the Reformation, to recapture the "purity," the structure, and the dynamism of the earliest Christian community. The radical reformers and those who followed their tradition were convinced that the church must be a *Gemeinde* and a *koinonia*.

Community and fellowship replaced sacramentalism in their view of the church, and while these concepts were not unique to them, they reinstated them with renewed intensity and priority. With the noteworthy exception of the Hutterites, the descendants of the Anabaptists have not practiced a pure communism. However, among the Amish and certain Mennonites the experience of community and fellowship is such that insurance and social security are rejected. Mutual aid and assistance extends to any member of the community who is in need. Thus, public assistance and insurance benefits are nonexistent. Communal assistance is perhaps most dramatically illustrated when a barn is destroyed by fire. This becomes the concern and responsibility not of the individual family concerned and their insurance company, but of the *Gemeinde*. The community gathers together and usually in one day a new barn is constructed. This is a "happening" which unites and strengthens the bonds of community.

When the plain people migrated to the New World they first settled in the Philadelphia area. Before long, however, they migrated westward, particularly to the Conestoga country which today comprises Lancaster County; and it is here that the largest concentration of the plain people is found. They became a rural people who developed and nurtured strong familial and communal ties. Their sectarian stance with its exclusiveness, together with their immobility and their relatively small population, further enhanced their close-knit communities. Almost without exception, marriage was between members of the community. After generations of intermarriage, the familial ties became quite pronounced. Today in the Amish and the Mennonite communities such names as King, Lapp, Fisher, Esch, Stolzfus, Martin, and Landis abound. Amidst the fertility and the beauty of the Lancaster County countryside they and their forebears have lived for almost 300 years. This has resulted in a communal stability, tradition, and heritage which is so at variance with the urbanized, technological, faceless, and mobile society in which many of us live.

Amidst the transciency of so many contemporary Americn communities, the Amish-Mennonite ones appear so abiding and permanent. To establish roots requires time and discipline and effort, and our constant mobility mitigates against it. Many of us suffer from the malaise of rootlessness. We experience an identity crisis, not knowing who we are or where we belong. But with the plain people it is otherwise. They have deep roots and they know who they are. They experience a communal solidarity and security that becomes so evident to outside observers. The traditions and sociological and psychological patterns which have evolved have set boundaries and are as signposts which define where one has come from and where one is going. There is little wonder, therefore, that choosing to leave such a community is a momentous decision which is not made effortlessly and painlessly.

This need to belong, to be accepted, and to be affirmed is universal. The apostle Paul said that no one lives to himself and no one dies to himself and that we are members one of another. Much of the turmoil of the 1960s and the subsequent turn toward communal living and eastern religions can be understood in this context. The rebellion against the establishment reflected this need for identity, for self-affirmation, for acceptance, and fellowship. And the turning away from Christianity to cults and eastern religions by many youth today may be an evidence of the same phenomenon. Christianity, as compared with eastern religions, is rationalistic. It has traditionally placed much emphasis upon doctrines and theological formulations which were rationally discerned. In the low church tradition, preaching the Word occupies the central focus of the worship, but this too is largely a rationalistic and intellectual exercise. In eastern religions there is an experiential dimension and a sense of mystery which may be lacking in most of the established churches. Moreover, one of the strong appeals of the cults is their encouragement of fellowship—of close and meaningful human relationships.

It is this community and fellowship that impresses the visitor to an Old Order Mennonite church. While it is difficult for an outsider to attend an Old Order Amish service, the fact that they meet in their houses, moving from one house to another each Sunday, is itself symbolic of the concept of *Gemeinde*. The church is a family and the houses in which families live become the church where brothers and sisters meet to praise God and affirm and accept one another.

The plain people have more often referred to their places of worship as meetinghouses rather than churches, and this is significant. The term "meetinghouse" has a two-fold implication. It, of course, is the place where the community regularly gathers to worship—to "meet" God. It has its counterpart in the Old Israel where the tabernacle was referred to as the "tent of meeting." But the meetinghouse has another purpose; it is the place where people meet each other. Going to the meetinghouse each Sunday is a spiritual experience where one meets God through prayer and praise and where one is instructed and challenged by the preaching of the Word. But it is also a social happening, an occasion where human ties are nurtured and deepened. From the perspective of an outsider, the latter appears to be as important and significant as the former.

For the plain people the church is the central institution. Given their lack of transportation and communication and their isolation, the church becomes not only the house of worship but also the center where news about members of the community is shared. Each Sunday becomes a sort of miniature family reunion. Many of the members are related to each other by virture of their isolated and stable community roots, but each is related to the other because each person is a member of the *Gemeinde*—the family of God and his Christ.

At various times I have worshipped in an Old Order Mennonite church, and these experiences have afforded a number of impressions and observations. For one, the Old Order groups represent the "purity of the tradition" from which the more progressive Mennonites, the Brethren, and the Brethren in Christ have to a lesser or larger degree departed. To enter an Old Order Mennonite meetinghouse grounds and buildings is to be transported back in time to a point where the now more progressive "plain people" once were. But through the process of acculturation the horse and buggies have given way to automobiles, the plain coats to lapels and neckties, the long hair and prayer coverings to short hair and bare heads, Pennsylvania German and German to English, the ministers' table to pulpits and divided chancels, the "uneducated, free" ministry to seminary-trained pastors, and the isolated meetinghouses to churches involved in the social, economic, and political problems of their communities.

An Old Order Mennonite meetinghouse is "striking" in its plainness and simplicity. One finds none of the traditional Christian symbolism. Except for its solid and careful construction there is no artistry or creativity—no carvings, pictures, curtains, floor coverings. Unlike most modern sanctuaries, the "pulpit" is in the middle of the long side of the church rather than the short side. Along the wall of the long side is a bench which is reserved for the ministers. In front of the ministers is the preachers' table from which the sermons are given. Extending out from the middle of the preachers' table is another table around which the men who lead the singing sit. The congregation is divided with women and girls on one side and men and boys on the other. Moreover, the various age groups sit in different sections of the meetinghouse. Small children stay with their mother or father but children from about kindergarten age up sit together in groups. The service lasts for two to two and a half hours. For me one of the most amazing features of the service is the discipline and behavior of the younger children who sit quietly without aid of books, paper and pencil, toys, etc. for the entire service. Their legs are too short to reach the floor and so they occasionally swing them, but there is no talking or undue commotion from them.

Behind the sisters' side of the house is a room through which they enter the church and to which they retire to take care of the babies who may be crying or otherwise need attention. As might be expected, the babies cry frequently during the service, and what would be regarded as distraction in many of our churches, is accepted as a normal pattern. The service is for the entire family and it is customary to bring infants to church as soon as they are old enough to be taken anywhere. Today most churches of other denominations have nurseries for babies and activities for small children during the worship hour. Thus, the adults can worship in peace and quiet, undeterred by the cries and antics of the young ones. But in a time when family solidarity and community are being seriously eroded, perhaps the scene of the whole family together in worship is a powerful and dramatic symbol. I remember one Brethren elder who used to say that a church service did not seem right or normal without a baby's cry. That statement may appear strangely out of place in many of our sophisticated and "stuffy" churches, but it may point to a dimension of *Gemeinde* that we have lost.

One of the serious problems in so many urban and suburban churches, as well as rural ones, concerns our seeming inability to experience meaningful fellowship and relationships. The goal of realizing *koinonia* seems to be an elusive one in spite of our "fellowship dinners," recreational activities, and small groups. The paradox is that among the "Old Orders" one feels an intensity of community in spite of the total lack of the usual techniques designed to strengthen the fellowship. One can give sociological reasons for this seeming paradox, but a large part of the answer is rooted in their lifestyle and value system. Industrialization and urbanization have tended toward isolating and separating people from each other rather than realizing deeper levels of community and solidarity.

The Amish and the Old Order Mennonite services are in Pennsylvania German and German. Pennsylvania German is spoken exclusively in the home, and in the past it was not unusual for a child to learn English only after beginning school. The language used in the house and meetinghouse is a tie and a community with the tradition of the past. Moreover, it is a further sign of separation from the world, of isolation from the wider culture. Forty and more years ago, Pennsylvania German was widely spoken in the Pennsylvania Dutch country, not only by the plain people but by the "church people" such as the Lutherans and Reformed. But today it is a dying language which most young people, with the exception of Amish and Mennonite, cannot speak or understand. So the use of Pennsylvania German in home and church serves to preserve the tradition and to mark those who use it as a "peculiar people."

Getting ready to go to church is a more involved experience for Amish and Old Order Mennonites than for most of us. The service begins at a relatively early hour, about 9:00 or 9:30 a.m. This means that the morning farm chores must be completed, breakfast must be prepared and eaten, everyone must dress in his or her "Sunday clothes," and the horse or horses must be harnessed and hitched to the buggy or buggies. The time to get to the house or church must be carefully calculated. This is especially true for the Amish who meet in different houses each Sunday. The Old Order Mennonites generally alternate between two or three different meetinghouses. The time required to get to church by horse and buggy is, of course, longer than it would be by automobile. Many of the younger boys and teenagers, as well as some girls, use bicycles to go to church. At any rate, by the time the stated time for the service arrives, practically everyone is present. The horses are tied in the sheds or outside to hitching rails. The sight of 200 or more horses and buggies in a churchyard is one not soon forgotten.

The service begins on time, punctuality being one of the prized Germanic and Pennslvania Dutch virtues. I remember a childless couple in my home church who were in the habit of being late for church. One time I heard the brother remark, "Better late than never," to which one of the elders replied, "Better not late at all." If there is a Germanic or Pennsylvania Dutch hierarchy of sins, tardiness must rank quite high.

The people assemble gradually before the service begins with those who arrive early fellowshipping and conversing both outside and inside the meetinghouse. The older people and the small children tend to take their seats in the meetinghouse first. They are followed by the teenage girls. Last of all, and just before the service begins, the teenage fellows take their places at the back of the meetinghouse. I am told that the young Amish men do the same, coming into the house at the last moment. The seating of the young men is never lost to the young women who view their arrival with more than detached interest. For it is in the context of the *Gemeinde* where young men and women meet and subsequently get married and rear their families. The church is the center, not only of their religious life, but of their social life as well. Indeed it is no exaggeration to note that for the Amish and the Mennonites the religio-social sphere is coterminous and indistinguishable.

The Old Order Mennonite service contains hymns which

are usually lined and the singing is started by the "singers" who sit in front of the ministers' table. The singing is slow and is sung from books containing only the words. The tunes are chosen and adapted by the "singers." There is an ethereal and moving quality about the hymn singing which conveys a transcendent and mystical dimension. There are two prayers for which the worshippers kneel, facing the backs of the benches. The first prayer is silent while the final one is audibly led by one of the ministers and is concluded with the Lord's Prayer. There are two sermons—an introductory one and the main one which lasts for an hour or more. The Scripture reading and the hymns are in high German which is considerably "Pennsylvania Germanized."

The sermons are in Pennsylvania German with an occasional phrase or sentence in "die andere Sprach"—English—and they are given without recourse to notes or manuscript. They are primarily expository and hortatory, consisting of biblical quotations and interpretation and of instruction on how to live the Christian life. Personal piety and ethics are stressed, and there is an absence of the social implications of the gospel. The themes of evangelism, missions, and outreach are minimized because these have little priority. The preaching has a definite apologetic purpose and character. The minister is responsible for defending and propagating the tradition and for conveying "sound doctrine." Moreover, his role is to warn the community against the pitfalls of *Hochmut* and worldliness and to encourage them to live a life marked by simplicity, integrity, and spirituality. A congregation has about three or four ministers, and after the main sermon each minister makes brief comments and further exhortation on it. The one who preached then gives a concluding response which is followed by announcements, a hymn, and the closing prayer. No offering is received during the service. If any emergency arises within the congregation or if work needs to be done on the meetinghouse, funds are collected for these specific purposes. Except for taxes on the property, the usual expenses incurred by established churches do not exist. There are no pastoral expenses, no utility and telephone bills, and no funds set aside for traditional outreach ministries.

Since the meetinghouses are rather sizable and there is no amplification, hearing the minister can be a problem, especially for those in the back of the house. The frequent cry of babies adds to this problem. Then, too, some ministers speak lower and more indistinctly than others. One gets the distinct impression that much of the speaking is not heard or paid attention to and that the children get little from the service. The preaching does not deal with specific psychological and social problems which may be troubling the members. It is marked rather by broad and general and often disjointed biblical exegesis and by admonitions to persist in and to perpetuate the traditions. One concludes that it is the meeting, the coming together, that is crucial and most significant. The horizontal dimension of love towards the neighbor appears to be as prominent as the vertical dimension of the worship of God. With the absence of symbolism and the negation of sacramentalism, the meeting of the community—the *Gemeinde*—takes on an unmistakable centrality. A further evidence of this orientation can be witnessed after the worship service ends. It is then that the "meeting begins." There is no rush for the exits or no anxiety about getting home for dinner or missing the next bus or subway. There is reflected rather a contentment, a peace of mind, and a simplicity of speech and manner which is strangely different from the complex and harried existence of so many of us. The period after the service is given to fellowship and to meeting anew those brothers and sisters who are members of the same household of faith. Eventually, the congregation disperses and one by one the buggies leave for the journey homeward or, as the case may more often be, to eat the noon meal and visit further with relatives or other members of the *Gemeinde*.

Apart from the weekly worship services, another strong bond of community has been the informal visiting which usually takes place on Sunday afternoons. These visitations require no invitation. Given the abundance of food and produce among the rural Amish and the Mennonites, unexpected company is not as much of a problem as it would be for most urban and suburban families.

This practice of Sunday visiting has largely been abandoned by the progressive Mennonites and the Brethren, probably to their detriment. There is something about eating and visiting together which makes the Sunday afternoon TV sports spectaculars a pallid substitute.

When I return to Lancaster County I sometimes buy potatoes from an Old Order Mennonite farmer. I was completely astonished when on one occasion he informed me that various families "open up" their place for young people's gatherings.

77

He told me that on the previous Sunday evening they had between 400 and 500 young people between the ages of 18 and 25 for supper. Imagine the logistics of "parking" the horses and buggies for that amount of people, to say nothing of the amount of food required! I did know that he at least had plenty of potatoes! This "happening" also impressed me with the fact that if young people represent the future church, then the future of the Old Order Mennonite is truly hopeful and secure.

Any discussion of community among the plain people must of necessity reckon with the centrality of the family. Strong and stable families have been the foundation of the plain society and of the church. Their view of the family has its rootage in biblical and ecclesiastical tradition. Marriage is ordained by God and according to Genesis is a part of God's creative activity. In the New Testament Jesus blesses marriage by his presence at the wedding in Cana. In the New Testament there are rather specific instructions regarding marriage, divorce, and remarriage. Marriage is not only a union between two individuals, but it is a social event. It takes place within the context of the body of Christ—the *Gemeinde*—and its members and their well-being are primary. Personal matters, even in family life, are secondary. One implication of this view of marriage was that marriage should be accomplished between members of the community, between those of "like precious faith." Thus, marriage with someone outside the church was greatly discouraged if not prohibited. And if such a "mixed marriage" should occur, the hope was that the outsider would join the *Gemeinde*.

Traditionally, families have been large, and among the more conservative groups church growth almost exclusively depended upon the families of the community. There was little or no attempt to evangelize outsiders. Large families were also a definite economic asset because everyone could be engaged in the multifarious aspects of farm life. The family structure was patriarchal in the early days as it still is among the more traditional groups. Both at home and in the church, men took the leadership and made the basic decisions. Discipline tended to be strict and in some cases so much so that self-development and realization were thwarted. In the church, women were seen but not heard since it was the men who led every part of the worship service. The influence of the women's liberation movement has been nil insofar as the Amish and the Old Order Mennonites are concerned.

Family stability has been a notable characteristic of the plain people. The home tended to be the center of social, recreational, and religious events. Given the strong ties between home and church and the subsequent social and psychological restraints which resulted, divorce, desertion, and separation were rare if not nonexistent. In more recent years, however, the wide-spread and frequent incidence of divorce in our society is making inroads among the Brethren and among the more progressive Mennonites as well. The Amish and the Old Order Mennonites remain exceptions to this pattern. The relentless and pervasive influence of urbanization, individualism, and secularism will continue to pose one of the gravest threats to the family stability of the plain people.

One of the evidences of family stability and solidarity is to be seen in the way Amish and Old Order Mennonites have cared for their aged and those who are physically or mentally handicapped. Rarely have they sent one of their own away to institutions for specialized care. They have assumed this responsibility themselves even at times when the demands exceeded their facilities or ability to cope with the situation. As noted earlier, they have not relied upon Social Security or insurance or institutional care. Their strong sense of community, of service, of caring, as well as their economic ability, have made them self-sufficient in the care for the aged, the handicapped, and the chronically ill.

Unlike the prevalent, contemporary nuclear family, the Amish and the Mennonite families are extended families, consisting of children, parents, grandparents, and perhaps great-grandparents. As older people come to the time of retirement or disability, they are not sent away to institutions, but room is made for them by their children. In many cases this involves an addition to the house so that they can have their own quarters and yet be in contact with their children and grandchildren. As one goes through the Amish area these "Grossdawdy" houses are much in evidence. Here is but one more example of the plain peoples' sense of familial and community solidarity and continuity. The interchange and the harmonious relationship between the generations with its potentiality for education, for imparting experience and wisdom, and for spiritual nurture is a blessing denied to the great majority of today's mobile, nuclear families.

The tradition of the plain people which I have attempted to reflect upon in this book has so many admirable, prudent, and positive aspects. It is a tradition with a long history. Moreover, it has had a significant influence upon the wider church's life and history. The descendents of the radical reformers have been influential in shaping the free church tradition with its emphases upon separation of church and state, the priesthood of every believer, and the inseparable relationship between creeds and deeds, faith and works, theology and ethics. Throughout its history this movement has kept before the Christian community the values of nonresistance and peacemaking, of service, of spirituality, and of fellowship and community. As must be evident by now, I am most sympathetic with, and have a very positive feeling toward, this branch of the Christian church because my spiritual nurture and outlook have been rooted in its life. One must conclude that without the salt and leaven and light provided by this movement the church of Christ would be the poorer. This Christ-against-culture stance is a necessary one, but as with every tradition, it is finite, partial, and in need of the judgment and correction of others.

To turn away from the world and to deny one's relationship to culture is to affirm in words what is denied in action. No one can give exclusive allegiance to Jesus Christ to the exclusion of culture. The claim of Jesus Christ is not upon a pure natural being—a child of nature—but upon one who has become human in culture. We are not only in culture, but the culture has penetrated us, many times in ways that we only dimly discern. We never come to maturity nor yet to faith in some sort of vacuum, but rather in a cultural milieu. We are members one of another not only in faith and devotion to Christ, but as inheritors of, and participants in, culture. We think as well as speak with the aid of the language of culture. Moreover, we have been surrounded by the science, economics, politics, and social customs of culture so that we can never extricate ourselves from these influences. We meet Christ as heirs of a culture which we cannot reject because it is a part of us.

For many of the plain people this inability to deny culture has been most evident in the economic realm. The economic system is a vital part of cultural heritage. It tends to reward those who invest wisely and who are diligent and thrifty. Consequently, many of the radical sectarians have benefited handsomely, and today the progeny of yesterday's martyrs and dispossessed are comfortable and quite wealthy. There is always

a tendency to except wealth and acquisitiveness from the cata-
log of worldly vices which are to be shunned. The dichotomy
between wealth and radical discipleship and the realization
that Jesus had "nowhere to lay his head" have been a persistent
and nagging dilemma for those who would eschew worldliness
and claim that Christ and culture can have no dealings with
each other.

But the problems attending the Christ-against-culture
position are not only in the area of ethics but also in theology.
There are several basic theological issues that this movement
poses. The question of the relationship between revelation and
reason and their respective potential for apprehending reality
is a problem for the radical sectarians. They tend to equate
reason with the methodology and the content of knowledge
which is to be found in the secular world or the culture.
Revelation is that Christian knowledge of God which is
centered in Jesus Christ and which is mediated to and pre-
served by the community of faith. Reason is the "wisdom of
this world" which is "foolishness with God" (1 Cor. 1:18-25).
The plain people have traditionally discouraged higher education. Amish young people still do not attend high school
because it would lead them away from the faith toward
worldliness. In this view, revelation is exalted and reason is
denigrated.

Another evidence of the subjection of reason to revelation
can be seen in the scepticism manifested toward theological
reflection and reasoning. As noted earlier, almost without exception the splits within the Mennonite movement have involved church discipline and order rather than doctrine. The
"theology of the schools" has had a low priority among them
except perhaps to caution against its "false doctrines." Ethics
and obedience to the order of the *Gemeinde* have taken
precedence over theologizing.

But here too, revelation or the "faith once and for all
delivered to the saints" comes to us within a cultural context.
Even though we accept the Protestant principle of the priesthood of each believer, nevertheless, we never confront the
biblical message or the historical Jesus alone. These have been
and are mediated to us through a community of faith which is
both historical and contemporary. What we experience and
what is "revealed" to us are determined to a large extent by
historical, sociological, and physchological considerations; in
a word, by cultural factors which we may not admit nor even

recognize. We can never leap the gap between ourselves and the Jesus of history and the primitive Christian community. We are surrounded by a "great cloud of witnesses" who have helped to shape what we know and experience. Thus the claim that we can be independent Christians or that we can apprehend Christ apart from culture is an impossible one. This means that the "revelation" we receive is always tinged with "reason," and the Christ who meets us can never be known in his fulness because of our finitude. And a vital dimension of that finitude is the relativity and the partialness of every theological and ecclesiastical system.

For the Christ-against-culture exponents this has meant that too often they have failed to acknowledge that their view of the faith was historically and culturally conditioned. Instead they have made absolute claims, and have equated with divine revelation beliefs and practices which were perhaps more the fruit of tradition and reason. For the radical Christians, the threat of idolatry is always present because there is the perennial tendency to equate "reason" with revelation—to invest finite practices and orders with ultimate meaning and significance.

Another theological issue involving the Christ-against-culture question has to do with the nature and prevalence of sin. For the plain people, sin and worldliness have always been closely identified. Sin resides in the culture, and to lead a pure and holy life is to separate oneself from the world. And how is worldliness to be understood? It is pride or *Hochmut* and is marked by such practices as the wearing of gaudy or immodest dress and jewelry. It is also characterized by resisting the discipline and disobeying the orders which define the boundaries of Christian discipleship. Worldliness or sin is also related to "worldly amusements" such as plays, shows, dancing, card playing, and of course sexual infractions. To live the good life and one "free from sin" is to refrain from these practices. Instead, one should cultivate spirituality by Bible reading, prayer, worship, and following the rules of the *Gemeinde*.

There is the tendency in this view to find the locus of sin outside the self in the world rather than within the self. To turn away from the world is believed to also be a turn away from sin. Sin's reality and power are due to the corruption of culture rather than to the corruption of one's fallen nature. According to the classical Pauline-Augustinian-Reformation view, sin is a pervasive power which perverts and distorts every area of one's existence. It is marked by a pride and an egocentricity which exalts the self, makes claims to independence, and denies one's dependence upon God and others. Carl G. Jung pointed to sin's essence when he spoke about our feelings of "godalmightiness."

By focusing upon the sins of the world, the Christ-against-culture advocates have perhaps minimized the reality of sin without the self. Pride has been equated with *sins* rather than with sin. This can easily lead to another sort of pride, one characterized by self-righteousness and premature claims to purity and goodness. If sin is love of the world, and goodness is turning away from the world, then my love of the self and its willingness to reject the world can easily become a manifestation of a new dimension of *Hochmut*—the latter perhaps being more demonic than the former. Those who would remain pure and "unspotted from the world" face the constant dilemma of confusing righteousness with self-righteousness.

Closely related to the question of sin is the relationship between law and grace. And this is especially pertinent for the radical sectarians. One of the common criticisms of them has been that they are legalistic and exclusive. They are the contemporary "Judaizers" who make Christianity into a new law and fail to see that it is a gospel for all persons. The tension between law and gospel, between works and faith, is weighted on the side of law and works. Discipleship is defined in terms of love of the neighbor, of modesty, and of nonresistance, and precise rules are formulated whereby one can judge the genuineness of one's Christian life. Those who conform to these patterns are a part of the true community of faith, while those who do not conform stand outside its borders. This emphasis upon conduct and good works can focus attention upon our will, our goodness, and our piety instead of the gracious work of God. Such exclusiveness can cause us to lose sight of the fact that God is at work among "other sheep who are not of this fold," and that we are members one of another to whom God in Christ has extended grace and forgiveness.

Perhaps the knottiest theological problem raised by the Christ-against-culture movement centers in the doctrine of creation or the relation of Jesus Christ to the Creator of nature. With their strong emphasis upon ethics, upon a practical Christianity, and upon law rather than gospel, there is the temptation among the radical Christians to convert their ethical dualism into an ontological division of reality. This bifurcation of reality is not unique with them but has a long history going back to Paul's flesh-spirit dualism and to the Marcion and Gnostic heresies of the early Christian period. The notion that the world of matter or flesh is the locus of evil and the demonic, while the realm of the spirit represents the essence of truth and goodness, runs counter to the view that *all* creation is good because God the Creator is its source and ground.

It was Augustine who above all others affirmed the goodness of creation. All that is is good because God the Creator is perfectly good. This is in keeping with the refrain running through Genesis 1: "And God saw that it was good . . . And God saw that it was very good." No part of God's creation is evil per se; evil results from human perversion of the good. Moreover, the New Testament affirms that God so loved the *world* that he sent his Son to redeem it, to restore it to its original state. And the doctrine of the Incarnation underscores the unity of the created order. The prologue of the Gospel of John affirms that the all-powerful, creative Word, which always existed, became clothed in flesh and entered history and dwelled among us. In the Incarnation God reaffirms the goodness of nature and his love for the world by "clothing himself in flesh" and by identifying himself with the world. Christ is savior of the world and the lord of history. God never abandons the world, even though humans have despoiled it, but he seeks ever to redeem and restore it. The eschatological vision foresees a time when all creation will be renewed and when there will be a "new heaven and a new earth."

The Christ-against-culture advocates, with their radical rejection of the world and their emphasis upon spirituality, are in danger of embracing a new gnosticism and of truncating the sweeping implications of God's creative, governing, and redeeming activity in his creation and incarnation. The Incarnation implies that God through Christ identified himself fully with all areas of human existence so that Jesus Christ was a "worldly" man to the fullest extent. The Anabaptist insistence upon discipleship — of *Nachfolge,* following after Jesus — leads to a separation from, rather than an affirmation of, the world. Jesus is not followed into the world but out of it into a "new community" which views culture as its enemy rather than as a part of God's good creation. The relation between Jesus Christ to nature and to culture becomes obscured. Rules and orders attempting to set bounds for nonconformity and the moral life, or certain spiritual principles, overshadow the full range of the person and work of the Jesus of history.

While turning away from culture in the name of Christ is an understandable and even necessary corrective to a "culture Christianity," nevertheless, it is a partial response, and perhaps its most serious theological problem lies in its distortion of the implications of God's creative and creating activity. The bifurcation between flesh and spirit, or between the world governed by a principle opposed to Christ and the spiritual realm guided by the spiritual God, evidences itself in a number of ways.

In the Amish and the Old Order Mennonite communities, the *Gemeinde* with its traditions and *Ordnung* tends to elevate community above individuality. This means that individual creativity and the cultivation of gifts and talents are sacrificed for the sake of the community. Worship is so circumscribed that there is no place for creative expression through art, instrumental music, solo and/or choral singing, drama and dance. These are all "worldly" and have no place in the worship of those who have been "called out of the world." How much artistic, musical, and leadership ability lies dormant because it is never cultivated and allowed to grow? In the times I have worshipped in Old Order Mennonite churches, I had to wonder why, for example, no flowers are ever brought into the church. Almost without exception, the plain people (especially the women) "love flowers," and their beauty and profusion lends an aesthetic dimension to their houses, lawns, and gardens, which is marvelous and beautiful. Is it "worldly" to bring flowers into the church "to God's glory?" If so, is this not an example of the denial of the goodness of God's creation?

There is a seriousness and somberness about their worship which seems to exclude spontaneity, celebration, and joy. There appears to be a suppression of emotion and somehow a truncation of the worship of God with "heart, soul, mind, and strength." But perhaps this is not wholly theologically and ecclesiastically conditioned. There may be ingrained in the Pennsylvania Dutch psychology the suppression of emotion, of feeling, of awe and wonder, and the exaltation of the "gods" of orderliness, efficiency, industry, and "seriousness."

The tradition of the Christ-against-culture position as exemplified by the Amish and the Old Order Mennonites has deep roots and has borne significant fruit. It is a needed corrective for much of contemporary Christianity. In the discussion above, I have attempted to underscore its strengths as well as to point out its inadequacies. Today the plain people have become a tourist attraction and are regarded by many as a quaint oddity. But in a time when "culture religion," "cheap grace," and a blatant secularism abound, it is encouraging, and yet a judgment upon us, to know that *the buggies still run*.

5

Chewing What You Can't Swallow

There is perhaps no issue which has been more ambiguous for the plain people than the growing and processing of tobacco. The tobacco grown in southeastern and central Pennsylvania is cigar-filler tobacco, commonly known as Pennsylvania Seedleaf, United States type 41.* Among the Pennsylvania counties where tobacco is grown, Lancaster County is by far the leading producer. The county has a variety of soils especially well-suited for the growing of cigar-filler tobacco.

The growing of tobacco has confronted the plain people with a peculiar moral dilemma. Its use has been discouraged if not condemned, and it is generally held to be detrimental to the Christian life. But as with other prohibitions, there are exceptions, and the smoking of cigars and the chewing of tobacco is not uncommon. However, there is no one who would encourage these practices as aids to more effective discipleship. A well-known Brethren evangelist used to say that he never liked to grow anything which he could not swallow after having chewed it.

Why then have the plain people persisted in growing tobacco when they have moral qualms about it? As is so often the case, when economic and moral considerations conflict, the former prevails. Tobacco is by far the best cash crop and thus yields the highest monetary return per acre. Due to the amount of labor required for growing and processing, tobacco acreage on a given farm is relatively small. It was not uncommon for a

---

*Much of the technical information in this chapter is taken from Orman E. Street, "Producing Cigar Tobacco in Pennsylvania," in *Farmers' Bulletin No. 2001, U. S. Dept. of Agriculture*. Washington, D. C.: Gov't. Printing Office, 1948, pp. 1-32.

farm youth or even an individual who lived in town to set out an acre or two of tobacco for the purpose of buying a car, of supplementing other income, or to realize other objectives.

The tobacco issue has long been a source of contention within Mennonite and Brethren churches. The more conservative elements in these groups are to be found in the "tobacco belt." The insistence upon conformity in dress, "sound doctrine," and "correct order in all things" were emphases found among the Mennonites and the Brethren of southeastern Pennsylvania. It was the "western" Mennonites and Brethren who were often suspect because of their innovative and more liberal practices. While the "easterners" often criticized the "westerners" for their "worldliness" and deviation from the "true faith," the latter often retorted by singling out the tobacco issue as a mark of moral inconsistency. The more recent findings on the detrimental effects of smoking set these problems in a new dimension and heighten rather than lessen the moral considerations and consequences.

While tobacco production is the most lucrative agricultural enterprise in southeastern Pennsylvania, it is also the most involved and time consuming. It is practically a year-round undertaking, and requires much time and many hands. While Lancaster County soil is conducive to the growing of tobacco, there may well be a secondary consideration involved. The plain people have had relatively large families, and tobacco became a family enterprise which involved everyone who was capable of working. From planting to cultivating to harvesting to getting the crop ready for marketing, there was ample opportunity to involve the entire family. Idleness and boredom, which are increasing problems for contemporary youth, were not much of an issue for families who had sizable tobacco acreage to keep them occupied. We often have been told that "idleness is the devil's workshop." If this is the case, how often was the devil thwarted by preoccupation and involvement with the "tobacco demon?"

In my hometown of Akron in Lancaster County, tobacco was very much in the picture. Before my time there were several cigar factories in Akron. When I was a boy there was still a cigar box factory in town, and we would get "box strips" there to make kite frames. Within town there were several tobacco sheds where the harvested tobacco was hung until it was cured. Akron was surrounded by farms where tobacco was the principal crop. One of the originial buildings of the

Mennonite Central Committee, which is located in Akron, was a former tobacco warehouse. Just west of Akron were two farms which were owned by a prominent Mennonite. For many years tobacco was grown there. When the owner died and the farms came under the control of his daughter and son-in-law, tobacco production ceased and was replaced by tomatoes and potatoes. The son-in-law was a well-known Mennonite layman who was influential in locating the Mennonite Central Committee in Akron. The transition from growing tobacco to growing tomatoes and potatoes on these two farms was a decision based upon ethical considerations and was rather widely discussed, both pro and con.

As noted above, tobacco production is a long and laborious operation. It begins in the spring with the preparation of the seed beds and sowing the seed. The beds are steamed, preferably in the fall, for weed and disease control. Seeding may be done by mixing the seed with fine soil, apple pomace, ashes, or cottonseed meal and broadcasting the dry mixture over the beds. Another method is to stir the seed in a spinkling can of water and carefully sprinkle the water and seed mixture over the bed. One farmer who formerly grew tobacco, but whose farm has now been "developed," told me that he still had the special sprinkling can which he used to seed his tobacco beds. Tobacco seeds are very small, about the size of granulated sugar granules, so that a small quantity will seed a large area. One-half ounce of cleaned seed is sufficient to seed 100 square yards of bed space. Seed is usually obtained by leaving a few tobacco plants in the field untopped, thus allowing them to "go to seed." After seeding, the beds are usually covered with muslin. Frequent watering of the muslin is advantageous for producing normal growth. When the plants are five to eight inches high they are ready for transplanting.

Setting the plants is done by a planting machine which employs a tank for water and has two low seats on either side of the planter shoe. Two persons ride the planter and set the plants. This is something of an art and is manifested in straight rows, uniform spacing, and upright positioning of the plants. Rows are 36 to 40 inches apart with the plants 24 to 28 inches in the row. A spacing of 26 inches in the rows and 40 inches between rows provides 6,000 plants per acre. In Lancaster County, tobacco can be planted from early in May to early in July, given the long growing season. Most of the planting is done from June 1 to June 20. Cultivation begins soon after transplanting and continues as long as the cultivator will pass through the row without damaging the leaves. Hand-hoeing is also necessary to loosen the soil which the cultivator may have missed. Cultivation has a two-fold purpose—to break the crust near the plants and to kill weeds.

An important operation in tobacco production is topping and suckering. Topping is the removal of floral parts and the upper part of the stalk. This procedure produces a profound change in the plant's activity. A plant that is not topped continues to grow in height and produces seed-stalks bearing flowers and seed pods. The lower leaves ripen normally, but the upper leaves will be progressively less ripe. After topping, the remaining leaves enlarge, becoming thicker and less pliable. It is desirable that all the tobacco leaves ripen at about the same time. Both climate and soil fertility determine the number of nearly uniform leaves that can be produced. The level of soil fertility and growing conditions will determine the amount of leaves to be left on a plant. Under ideal conditions as many as 16 leaves can be left, while as few as 10 to 12 can be left under adverse conditions.

The imbalance produced in the plant by topping manifests itself in the development of suckers which are branches growing out of the axils of the leaves. The use by the suckers of the nitrogen and mineral elements furnished by the roots permits the leaves to ripen. In some cases suckers are removed only once before cutting. However, if the growth is profuse, suckering twice may be justified. At any rate, there should be no suckers on the plants when they are harvested because they interfere with proper curing.

About three or four weeks after topping, the plants are ready to harvest. The normal harvesting season is from August 20 to September 20. The tobacco stalks are cut with longhandled shears. Cutting is best done when the plants are dry and the weather clear. After the plants are wilted (usually about an hour after cutting) they are strung on four-foot hardwood laths to which an iron spear point is attached to one end. The spear end of the lath is set upright with the other end resting on the ground. The plants are speared through about five inches from the butt with five or six plants being strung on each lath. The laths are placed in rows on the ground, then loaded on wagons fitted with racks. Each wagon holds about 100 laths. The tobacco is hauled to the shed or barn where the laths are passed upward to workers who place them on poles. The laths should be spaced at least eight inches in order to prevent shed damage.

After the tobacco is hung in the shed the curing process which had already begun in the field continues at a more rapid rate. During the curing process more than 80 percent of the green weight is lost. Proper curing of tobacco is very crucial and is dependent upon favorable temperature and humidity conditions. Many tobacco farms in Lancaster County have tobacco sheds equipped with ventilating slats to more readily control temperature and humidity. However, most of the tobacco is cured in the large barns which are so prominent a feature of the southeastern Pennsylvania rural scene. These barns may house cattle, horses, pigs, and chickens and also contain such other farm produce as hay, straw, grain, and feed. Since these barns were not specifically or exclusively designed for tobacco, there is always danger of inferior quality tobacco due to shed burn, pole sweat, smothering, and other hazards. Before hanging tobacco in a shed or barn some farmers construct outdoor frames in the field and allow the tobacco to cure outside for a period of about a week or 10 days. This minimizes some of the critical problems attending shed curing.

By far the most time-consuming aspect of tobacco production is stripping the crop. This is the tobacco farmer's winter occupation and lasts from late fall until early March. Before tobacco is stripped it is removed from the curing shed and hung in a damp cellar for several days. This must be done on damp days or the tobacco will be too dry to handle. After it is sufficiently moist to handle without breaking, the laths are brought into the stripping room and the stalks are removed. Both the damp cellar and the stripping room are beneath the curing shed, thus affording ready access to the tobacco hanging in the shed. The leaves are removed from the stalk, and they are sized in boxes containing compartments varying in length from 16 to 32 inches in two-inch intervals. The leaves are then tied into "hands" containing about 15 leaves, a shorter leaf used as a tier. These various sizes are packed together in a bale which is covered with paper (expect for the butt ends) and tied with three or four strings. Each bale weighs about 70 pounds. The bales are then stored until sold to a buyer. After the crop is sold it is taken to a warehouse where further processing (fermentation and sweating) take place. Finally, the process is culminated by the manufacture of cigars and chewing tobacco.

More recently there have been changes in the processing of tobacco which make the stripping operation easier and less time consuming. The leaves are stripped off the stalks and are not sized as formerly. They are tied in bundles and baled. The reason for this change is that the tobacco leaves are now ground and the ground tobacco is rolled into sheets from which wrappers are cut for the making of cigars. The new procedure utilizes the tobacco ribs which formerly were thrown out. There are several advantages with the new procedure: it is faster, it is less wasteful, and more "perfect" cigars can be made from the rolled sheets than from the leaves.

From the above, it is very evident that tobacco growing is a tedious and difficult process. In addition to the uncertainties of climate conditions, tobacco diseases and injuries are always a serious threat and at times lead to substantial loses for the tobacco farmer.

As noted earlier, tobacco was a basic element in Akron's economy. A sizable percentage of the population was dependent upon tobacco in one way or another for livelihood. I can well remember that "tobacco talk" was prevalent wherever people gathered—in stores, at sales, and in church. Comments about the weather, planting, the progress in stripping, selling, and other aspects of tobacco farming were general topics of conversation. While I never worked with tobacco, I would often get into the sheds and stripping rooms. The odor (or shall one say, aroma) emanating from these structures is unforgettable. Moreover, the long hours that family members spent together in the stripping rooms were bound to form strong communal ties and lasting memories. Here truly were unparalleled opportunities for reflection and conversation among family members and working colleagues whose age spans stretched from teenage to elderly.

As might be expected, cigar smoking was not uncommon in Lancaster County; neither was chewing. One former Brethren farmer related how his father prepared his year's supply of chewing tobacco. After sweating the tobacco, he boiled birch roots which have a distinct wintergreen flavor. He then poured this liquid over the tobacco. Thus he had wintergreen-flavored chewing tobacco—quite an innovative accomplishment! I cannot vouch for this, but I was told that at times before entering an Old Order Mennonite meetinghouse the men, having extinguished their cigars, lined them up on an outside windowsill. There is little wonder that cigar tobacco, which has had so central a place in Lancaster County's agriculture, should be a chief topic of concern and conversation and should even develop its own folklore.

In recent years, tobacco production in Lancaster County has declined, and more and more farmers are turning to dairying or beef cattle. One reason for this must be the prodigious amount of time and work involved in tobacco growing and processing. Uncertainties about climatic conditions may be a lesser consideration. As one friend who is a feed salesman and has wide contacts with farmers noted, with dairying and cattle the farmer has everything in or around the barn; the work is more tidy and less time consuming and the situation in general is more predictable and manageable. Another consideration may be the decline in cigar smoking and tobacco chewing which is evident in our population. Cigar smoking is now banned on airlines and in many public places and is generally considered more offensive than either cigarettes or pipes. As for chewing, it has rough sledding in a more urbanized, genteel, and sophisticated culture.

One would like to think that the decline of tobacco growing by the plain people is a sign of sharpened moral sensitivity. With the increasing evidence that smoking is hazardous to one's health, it would appear that a new dimension has been added to the pros and cons of tobacco production. It is always difficult to probe the question of motivation. Here and there tobacco farming has been and is being abandoned because of ethical considerations, and this may be an increasingly significant trend. But in many cases, one must conclude that such decisions are motivated more by economic, pragmatic, and utilitarian, rather than moral and religious concerns. At any rate, whatever the future prospects of tobacco, there is little doubt that its place in the historical and sociological background of Lancaster County's agricultural community is pronounced and secure. And as with most ethical issues, the choices involved have just enough ambiguity that one can rationalize any qualms of conscience and continue to grow and produce that which can be chewed but not swallowed.

6

A City Set on a Hill

The town of Akron is about 11 miles northeast of Lancaster and it was there that I was born and grew up. In my youth, Akron had a population of about 700 and was largely clustered on the top of a hill from which one could get a good view of the surrounding countryside. All around the town were farms on which tobacco was grown as the chief cash crop. Akron's prime landmark was a 100-foot stand pipe which was visible from a long distance in every direction. Route 222 between Lancaster and Reading snaked its way in and out of Akron and came through the square. Later the highway was relocated about one block west of the square.

Today there is a new four-lane Route 222 which bypasses Akron to the east and which cuts a swath through some of Lancaster County's choicest land. The quietness and pastoral quality of a former day is now punctuated by two concrete ribbons along which hundreds of cars and trucks travel each day. Where once the stillness was disturbed by the sound of an occasional horse's hoofs, there is now the almost constant din of highway traffic. An Old Order Mennonite whose farm was bisected by the new highway related that when the wind comes from the south, the roar of the big diesel trucks disrupts the peace and tranquility of the night. What the great majority would term "progress," the plain people see as but one more intrusion by the "world" into their homogeneous community.

It was Mark Twain who said that the older he got the more vividly he remembered things that never happened. To romanticize the past, to minimize or even forget its hardships and failures, and to remember instead its joys and successes, appears to be a universal trait. In retrospect the snows are deeper, the summers hotter, the fish bigger, and the work harder. So as I attempt to remember and to reflect upon the past, I too am bound to "remember things that never happened." Moreover, what one recalls is seen and filtered through tinted lenses. Our biases, prejudices, and subsequent experiences to a large degree determine what we see and remember and how we interpret these experiences. We can never perceive the *ding an sich,* the thing in itself. Rather, our perceptions and recollections are partial and limited in their perspective. In the area of historiography, detachment and objectivity must always remain "impossible possibilities." The existentialist denial of the Hegelian claim to historical objectivity was a much-needed corrective. History is not an objective and exact science. Rather, it is enmeshed in both the grandeur and the misery of human existence, with its passion, anxiety, and despair, as well as its hopes and aspirations. Likewise, the one who would write and interpret history brings to the task these same qualities, and they determine to a large extent what he or she sees. Event and interpretation are always integrally related. Historical events do not come to us out of some pristine, objective milieu. Rather, we receive them as they are remembered and interpreted for us by those whose own existential situation determines what is seen.

The historical process of attempting to recover and interpret the past is also conditioned by wide-ranging psychological considerations. Freudian psychology has maintained that no experience is lost to us, but that it is all "stored" in the subconscious mind. What we can normally recall is only a small segment of the whole. It is like an iceberg with only a small part of the entire mass extending above the surface. The largest and potentially most dangerous disruptive part lies below the surface and is not visible. So it is with our ability to recall the past. The unpleasant, the disturbing, the threatening, is "forgotten" and lies buried in that amorphous, unconscious realm. But sometimes in unforseen and uncalculated moments, out of this abyss there erupt memories which disturb our peace and threaten our psychological equilibrium. By and large, we "remember" the pleasant and pleasurable experiences—those which both create and affirm our presuppositions and which enhance our egos. So it is not at all unusual that we "remember things that never happened," and that we mask our finitude and our biases by false claims to impartiality and objectivity.

The Akron of my childhood and youth was a relatively homogeneous Pennsylvania Dutch community. There were no blacks, no Jews, and few Roman Catholics. The prevailing Protestantism was composed of sects which emerged from the German Reformation. These were Lutheran, Evangelical, Evangelical Congregational, Zion Children's (Brethren in Christ), and the Church of the Brethren. Today, except for the most recent establishment of a Bible Baptist Church, a General Conference Mennonite Church, and the merging of the Evangelical Church into the Evangelical United Brethren and now the United Methodist Church, these sects still predominate. For a number of years there was an Assembly of God Church in Akron, but it has now moved outside of town. With Akron's mushrooming growth since World War II and the increasing industrialization of Lancaster County, the town's population has become much more heterogeneous. Akron is still overwhelmingly "white," but its religious constituency is more diverse.

Politically, Republicanism predominated. Democrats were a "rare and suspect breed." One long-time resident of Akron told me that there was a time when he could count the Democrats on one hand. Although Republicans are still in the majority, today the numerical imbalance between the two parties is not nearly so pronounced as formerly.

Akron's major industry is a shoe factory which across the years has had its struggles. I would suppose that at one time or another a majority of Akron's residents were employed there. Prior to World War II, as many as 700 persons worked in the shoe factory which manufactured women's shoes. During this period the daily production was about 10,000 pairs. Today, the operation is more automated and the number of people employed and the production much less. I worked in the shoe factory for several years and was a stitcher at the time I left to enter the Civilian Public Service program during World War II. Since its founding, the factory was controlled by a few local families. It has never been unionized and, as I recall it, the atmosphere was more than a little tinged with paternalism. The minimum wage was 35¢ per hour when I began working, and there were no vacations and no provision for sick leave or retirement benefits. From the 35¢ rate, one was "promoted" to a piece-work operation where the rate of pay was a certain amount per case of shoes for a given operation. A case consisted of 36 pairs of shoes. The rates for the respective operations never appeared to be too equitable, so that some workers would receive considerably more per day than others even though the time and energy expended were relatively the same. It was a competitive system in which it was always tempting to try to beat one's working colleagues. The Pennsylvania German term for this was "rausing" which means to work fast and furiously. These were the days before the institution of the coffee break, and except for the tobacco smokers, workers would work straight through from morning to lunch and from lunch to quitting time in the evening. My father worked in the shoe factory for many years before his retirement. Two of my uncles were foremen. During the Great Depression, the factory continued to operate, and while our family was never affluent, we came through the Depression without suffering the wrenching and traumatic economic privations which so many families experienced.

In addition to the shoe factory, there was a shirt factory in Akron. After some years it closed and a heel factory began operation. But these industries were much smaller than the shoe factory. My mother worked in the shirt factory for a number of years during my childhood, and I was taken care of by my maternal grandmother who lived with us until her death at the age of 88. My grandmother's sister lived next door to us. The two of them always conversed in Pennsylvania German, and so I learned to understand it without difficulty.

Akron had two grocery stores which were not only business but also social centers. Given the small size of the town, everyone knew everyone else and the stores were choice centers for socializing and acquainting oneself with the latest news. This was before the packaged and frozen food era. Many items were "loose" and had to be weighed out. There were no self-service and no check-out areas, and one waited in line to be served by one of the clerks. This also predated the ubiquitous paper bags for transporting groceries, and most people used baskets for carrying them.

The square at Akron was bounded by one of the stores, by a bank, by a hotel, and by an apartment house, as it was called then. Next to the store was a small building which housed the post office. Mail was delivered to and from the railroad station which was about a mile from town. In those days "junk mail" was at a minimum, and it was always an exciting experience to receive a piece or two of mail.

The bank was the place where the shoe factory checks were cashed and where one would make small deposits from meager earnings. As I look back now, I am amazed how quick and efficient the service was compared with the computerized urban and suburban banks I now visit.

On another corner of the square was the hotel which sold food and refreshments and after the repeal of the Prohibition Amendment added beer to its fare. While many of the townspeople objected to the sale of alcoholic beverages, there was widespread agreement that the hotel was run in an orderly manner and that Akron was free from many of the problems attending other such establishments. The hotel has since been razed and replaced by a self-service grocery store, and to the delight of some and the dismay of others, Akron is now "dry."

Among my memories of the hotel are the croquet games which were played on the adjoining lawn, the medicine shows that sometimes set up there in the summer, and one young man's attempt to "break the record" for the number of hours rocked in a rocking chair. For some years I distributed the *Reading* (Pa.) *Eagle* newspaper in Akron. The papers were dropped off daily at the hotel by bus.

As long as I can remember there was a restaurant in Akron. It changed hands and even locations, but I recall it as a place where older and younger residents of the town would gather — the younger perhaps to go for a drive somewhere, while the older men would talk and just loaf. During one proprietorship of the restaurant, it was noted for its homemade ice cream. Within recent years the Akron Restaurant has moved into spacious quarters just south of town along the old Route 222. It now has a deserved reputation as one of the best dining places for Pennsylvania Dutch food, and patrons come from far and wide to enjoy its fare.

Akron had several cigar factories which processed the tobacco grown in the surrounding areas. There was also a box factory which made cigar boxes. It was that factory where we boys went to get box strips from which we made kite frames.

Judged by contemporary standards, Akron's housing was modest but adequate. The greatest percentage of the houses were frame construction with a small number of brick. During the 1930s, many houses were not equipped with indoor plumbing and consequently there were outside privies. I suppose one has never really lived if he or she has not visited an outdoor privy on a cold, windy, winter morning. That is an experience not soon forgotten! I recall that some privies were equipped with Sears Roebuck catalogs which were there for more practical and immediate purposes than shopping by mail or lusting for the latest fashions.

In many cases water was pumped by hand from outside wells. Except among the more conservative plain people, electricity became an accepted and welcome improvement. Its use paved the way for the replacement of coal oil lights by electric lights, of easing the traditional Monday washday by the use of electric washing machines instead of those turned by hand. Electric refrigerators slowly replaced the ice boxes, and this opened the way for the revolution that the frozen foods industry was to effect in the handling and preservation of food. The visit of the ice man several times a week is a vivid memory of my childhood, and only after I was a teenager did we have an electric refrigerator.

In the course of my childhood and youth our family lived at two locations in Akron. The first was a row house consisting of four houses joined together. We lived in one of the end houses. It was equipped with electricity and with a spigot in the kitchen. In the kitchen was a large "cook stove" which was fired by hard coal. Hard coal was the predominent fuel because Akron was within a reasonable distance of the Pennsylvania anthracite fields. In the "middle room" there was a heating stove from which a pipe went upstairs through one of the bedrooms into the chimney. The heat radiating from this pipe provided the heat for the second floor. As might be expected, sleeping in the winter was definitely on the cool side. The Pennsylvania Dutch quilts, which today are sought after as collectors' items, were necessities during the rigorous winters of yesterday.

In the 1930s the telephone was not the common instrument that it is today. We had no telephone until I was of high school age. If there was an emergency or some other good reason to use a phone, it was common to go to a neighbor or acquaintance who had one.

The technological innovation which was the most exciting was the radio. We did not have a radio until a number of years after they came into general use. But I vividly recall how I would go the next-door neighbor to hear Amos and Andy who followed Lowell Thomas each evening at 7:00 o'clock. This was a fascinating and almost mesmerizing experience. Later, after we got our own radio, I became an addict to the likes of not only Amos and Andy but also Jack Armstrong the All-American boy, Buck Rogers in the 21st century, the Singing

Lady, the Shadow and others. In a different vein, I remember how my father and I would listen on Sundays to the Catholic Hour with Monseigneur Fulton J. Sheen as the speaker and to National Vespers with Dr. Harry Emerson Fosdick. Maybe this was the origin of my life-long interest in great preachers and preaching. In all probabilty, radio newscasts by such commentators as Lowell Thomas and others generated in me an interest in politics and current events which persists to the present.

There was a sort of awesome and spell-binding attraction to hearing a radio for the first time. It was a source of amazement bordering on the miraculous to reflect on the possibility of transmitting sound without wires. I remember after we got our first radio, which was a large console type, I would occasionally look behind it to check whether there was anybody there.

Going to school is a major event in the life of a child, and next to the family it exerts a greater influence than any other institution. The Akron School consisted of eleven grades, and there were five teachers plus the principal who was both a supervisor and a teacher. There was no busing in those days. All the students had to walk to school. Neither were there any "frills" — no gymnasium, no auditorium, no vocational training such as shop and home economics, no drivers education, no sports teams, no clubs, no band — only the basic studies such as reading, penmanship, mathematics, history, science, English, Latin, German. Summer vacations were long by today's standards, extending from the end of April to the beginning of September.

As I look back on those days now, I realize that we were blessed with competent and dedicated teachers, and while the extracurricular activities were at a minimum, we did get good orientation in the basics. With the current longer school year, the elaborate buildings and equipment, and the many educational opportunities available to today's youth, there does not appear to be a noticeable upsurge in academic achievement. Rather, one hears all too frequently about high school graduates who have difficulty reading, writing, and performing simple mathematical problems. According to some reports, it appears that the present generation will be the first one in American history not to excel its parents in academic attainment.

Spelling was always one of my favorite endeavors, and I became rather proficient at it. On my way to school I would often meet a neighbor lady who was out sweeping her pavement. Many times she would ask me to spell various words and was favorably impressed with my responses. Of those she asked me, the two I still remember are "rhinoceros" and "hippopotamus."

Occasionally, spelling bees were held in the Akron fire hall as well as in surrounding communities. There were usually spelling classes and one class in "general information." These events were publicized and would attract good spellers from a fairly wide area. Prizes (usually books) were given to the three best spellers in each class. While still in grade school I won several prizes and relished the accolades of the audience who wondered that someone so young had successfully competed against adults.

Since Akron had only a three-year high school program, those students who wished to get a four-year diploma had to go to Ephrata High School, about two miles from Akron, for their twelfth year. This resulted in the unique situation of having two commencements—one at Akron and the other at Ephrata. The transition from Akron to Ephrata was not an easy one for several reasons. In our Akron graduating class there were about ten students, while at Ephrata there were more than 100. Given the immobility of the Akron community, I went to school for eleven years largely with the same persons. But at Ephrata everyone was strange, and the size of both the building and the student body was somewhat overwhelming. Moreover, no transportation was provided for us. Consequently, a number of us would usually hitchhike back and forth, as well as walk considerable distances.

Adequate economic security is a perennial problem for most of us, and during the Great Depression it reached crisis proportions. But as noted earlier, the shoe factory continued to operate, and while money was never plentiful, Akronites did not suffer undue privation. The period of the wide-spread use of credit and of the proliferation of advertising and consumer goods was still in the future. As I recall, there was a prevailing philosophy that one waited until the money was available before purchasing a given item. Credit was not encouraged as it is today. Thus there was more of a "doing without" if the money was not at hand. One example that left an impression upon me related to one of our neighbors. Automobile license plates cost ten dollars per year, but after July 1 they could be bought for five dollars. This neighbor would let his car set until after July 1 when he would buy the license at the reduced rate. Today, such an action seems almost incredulous.

Wages were low in the 1930s, but so were prices. Today's wage scales, as well as the inflated economy, could not even have been envisioned then. There was a barber in Akron who was a sort of combination of homespun philosopher and prophet. It has been my observation that barber shops are rather unique "centers of learning" and often provide "expertise" in such varied disciplines as political science, religion, economics, gambling, and sexuality. At any rate, my barber friend in Akron once made the "outlandish prophecy" to my father that one day his son would earn $10,000 per year. Such a statement then defied the bounds of credulity.

My father and I would occasionally go to various farms to buy a chicken or some other fowl, and then take it home to prepare it for the table. On one occasion we bought chickens for eight cents per pound. The cheapest gasoline I remember was seven gallons for a dollar. A farmer who lived just outside of town delivered milk which was dipped from a milk can into your container. The price was six cents per quart. Those were the days when you could buy candy for one cent, ice cream cones and soft drinks for five cents. Compared with current prices, rents and housing were unbelievably low. For many years we rented a house for $11 per month and when my father finally bought one, he paid $3,200 for it. For eight to ten thousand dollars one could have bought quite a mansion. I recall that my parents would send me every month with the $11 to pay the landlady. For that she would always give me a nickel.

Like any other community, Akron reflected the achievements and the foibles which characterize the human existence. Only a small minority of young people went to college. One time, when I was probably about 12 years of age, a local youth who was home from college for the summer was talking to some of us at the baseball diamond. He described his experiences, but the "world of academe" seemed so foreign to me I suspected that I would probably never enter it. Neither of my parents were high school graduates, and discussions about higher education and academic matters were not a part of my upbringing.

Akron had its eccentrics and town "characters." As long as I can remember, there was one especially who was teased but who could give as well as take. He was "different" and he was always one of Akron's best-known and "outstanding" citizens.

103

There was another who would wear an overcoat during the summer and who would check at the post office daily for his "big, fat letter," which seemingly never came. There were those whom today we would call alcoholics, but who were then referred to by more derogatory terms. There were those who lived together unmarried, and though homosexuality was a largely unknown and mysterious realm, at least one person in Akron had "come out of the closet." There was an occasional suicide with all its wrenching trauma. But unlike today, I cannot remember any young people attempting to take their lives. There was at least one financial scandal when the cashier of the bank was found guilty of embezzlement and was sentenced to the penitentiary. The most gruesome scene I remember involved several people who were on their way to Gettysburg. Just below Akron their car overturned and caught fire and they were burned to death. For some reason unknown to me, the local undertaker laid the charred bodies on the lawn and people came by to see them. The memory of that event is still vivid today even though it occurred more than 40 years ago.

Crime was almost unknown in Akron. Many people kept their doors unlocked day and night. An occasional theft might occur, but compared with today the situation was almost utopian. As a youth I knew nothing about such drugs as marijuana, cocaine, heroin, or the barbituates and depressants which are so much a part of today's scene. Then as now, nicotine and alcohol were the chief drugs. Like many boys, we would occasionally go "behind the shed" and smoke a cigar or cigarette. But I was never tempted to indulge in alcohol.

The long summer vacations were carefree and times for playing and having fun with friends. Some of the time was given to fishing either at the ice dam just below town or in the Cocalico Creek which was a bit farther. While the big ones always seemed to get away, it was nevertheless a good participatory recreation. Swimming was another activity which occupied quite a few of the summer hours. There was a dam breast across the Cocalico Creek and above it the water was fairly deep and wide. There was a swing suspended from one of the trees on which we would glide out across the water and jump or dive into the creek. We would walk or occasionally get a ride to the swimming hole. In later years, Ephrata built a disposal plant upstream, and that ended the swimming. Today, there is a trailer court in what was once the meadow through which we walked to our swimming site. Between

Akron and Ephrata is a dairy which has sold ice cream and dairy products for many years. I remember the day it opened for business. It was in the summertime, and on our way to swim we stopped and got free ice cream cones which were a part of the opening promotion. Among our other summer activities were playing baseball, flying the kites which we made, hiking in the fields and through the woods, and just "goofing off."

When fall and winter came a few of us boys would trap skunks within the confines of the borough. This obviously presented problems for the people around whose houses we trapped, as well as for our own families, because when one catches a skunk it becomes public knowledge in a short time. It was in connection with one of our skunk trapping endeavors that I had one of life's most frightening experiences.

Near our home was a cemetery, and another boy and I set traps around a shed which was used to store implements and materials needed for working in the cemetery and around the church. Before going to bed we decided to check our traps to see if we might have caught anything. It was dark and unbeknown to us, two men who were neighbors followed us and went into the cemetery near the shed. Just as we got to our traps there emanated from the cemetery a blood-curdling "oooo! oooo! oooo!" I was carrying the only flashlight we had, and I immediately began to run as fast as I could toward home, leaving my friend to stumble around and find his way as best he could. After getting home we learned what had happened. It was a great joke our neighbors played on us, and quite ingenious, but one that makes one's hair stand on edge and is remembered for a lifetime.

Before they were displaced by buses, trolleys were one of the major means of transportation, not only within urban centers, but also between cities and towns. Akron was on the trolley route between Lancaster and Reading. Before my time, the trolley route was about a mile east of town. A cement pavement led from town to the trolley station. This pavement went down a hill outside of town and was a favorite place for roller skating. Today, it is no longer used and is grown over with weeds and trees so that it is barely visible. Since automobiles were not as plentiful in those days, many people used the trolley to go shopping, either to Ephrata or Lancaster. For seven cents one could ride the two miles to Ephrata. As I recall, the eleven-mile ride to Lancaster cost 30 or 35 cents.

The trolley tracks also afforded "hiking routes" out of town, and walking on the ties or trying to see how long one could walk on the rails were favorite pastimes. While trolleys have not completely passed from the scene, and there is evidence of their renaissance, they recall a pre-air pollution era and one marked by a more leisurely mode of transportation and a less harried pace of life.

While automobiles had been around for a long time by the 1930s, yet there was a mystique and fascination about them for a young boy. I was about eight years of age when my father bought his first car. It was an Overland touring car which meant that it was open on the sides and fitted with curtains which could be closed in cold or rainy weather. Father bought it from another Akron resident for the exorbitant price of ten dollars. It was parked on the street in front of our house and on occasion, when father was at work, some of us boys would push it back and forth on the street and "play with it." From the Overland we graduated to a 1932 Chevrolet coupe. One of my fondest memories of that car was a trip our family took to northern Pennsylvania one Fourth of July weekend. We must have travelled more than 400 miles that weekend and that seemed to me then to be a major trip. This was the time before the interstate highways and the motels. Roads were narrow and quite curvy in many cases, and travel was considerably slower than it is now. Lodging was in tourist homes, of which there were many, or in modest cabins which were the precursors of today's motels.

Today, a trip from Akron to Lancaster or even to Philadelphia, which is about 60 miles distant, is commonplace and routine. But in the earlier days it was not so. In my youth, going to Philadelphia conjured up un image comparable to traveling from Akron to Chicago or St. Louis today. I recall that a number of the Akron baseball fans would go to Philadelphia, perhaps once a year, to see the professional Philadelphia Athletics play. I always envied them and regarded their adventure as a major undertaking.

Each fall "Farmers' Days" were held in Ephrata, Lititz, New Holland, and Manheim. These were a conglomeration of farmers' displays, carnival, and fair. They usually ran from Tuesday through Saturday and drew sizable crowds from a wide radius. While agriculture was the basic emphasis of Farmers' Days and produce, poultry, horses, and handicrafts were displayed and judged, the major attractions for many were the rides, shows, and games where the prizes were usually frustratingly elusive. At times these events provided a political forum prior to national and/or local elections. I have a vivid recollection of Henry Wallace speaking at the Ephrata Farmers' Day during the presidential campaign of 1936. He was a colorful and dynamic speaker and he left an impression upon me. Many years later, during his retirement years in Connecticut, I heard him again when he came to the Yale Divinity School where I was a student.

With the coming of winter and the anticipated snows, Akron was a good place to be for sledding or coasting. Since Akron was situated on a hill, coasting was good in any direction; but the favorite course began at the schoolhouse and extended for almost a mile down to the train station and beyond. I spent many an enjoyable evening coasting there. We used to "race" to see whose sled was faster and could go the farthest. Sometimes we would "hitch" a ride back up the hill by holding on to the bumper of an automobile. If there were quite a few sleds to be pulled, those who held on to the bumper would hook their feet in a sled behind them and thus form a sort of "sled train." These experiences remain most vivid even to this day.

When I was growing up in Akron, the population was small and homogeneous. One got to know personally practically everyone. What one did was not only his or her own business but was quickly known and became the business of everyone. Such an environment produced distinctive moral implications as compared with the dehumanization and anonymity characteristic of contemporary urban and suburban centers. The small-town atmosphere placed subtle restraints upon one's behavior. If one misbehaved or departed significantly from community mores, this became the "talk of the town" and was soon known by one's parents and relatives.

Ethnically, Akron was predominently Pennsylvania Dutch. I realize that it is difficult to generalize and to categorize any given group of people, but there appear to be certain Pennsylvania Dutch traits which set them apart. And while there are and were always glaring exceptions, the people I knew best reflected certain features which I know have had an impact upon my way of thinking and doing.

Thrift was a trait that was much prized and emphasized. To save, conserve, and even horde things was a widespread practice. For many, money was not to spend but to save. The reluctance to buy on credit was a reflection of this view. "Shopping around" and looking for bargains, while by no means confined to the Pennsylvania Dutch, was nevertheless one of their valued traits. Thrift and acquisitiveness were often equated with godliness and evidence of God's favor and ranked high in the hierarchy of moral virtues.

Closely related to thrift is industriousness or plain hard work. Surely among the Pennsylvania Dutch laziness and idleness were among the "sins" most condemned. While work was virtuous, I am sure that for some it became an escape from problems, just as alcohol or other drugs do for others. Nevertheless, being busy and working from morning till night was not the exception but more generally the rule. This view can readily lead to prideful individualism and the claim that "I worked for what I got." Moreover, it can induce deep feelings of guilt if one engages in leisure and recreational activities. The restless feeling and the compulsive notion that I should be "doing something" makes it difficult for many Pennsylvania Dutch persons to enjoy a vacation. There is something "wrong" with play and leisure because work is the superior and greater good. It also implies that one is self-reliant, self-sufficient, and does not depend upon others for anything.

I remember one woman who was always a hard worker and who was temporarily laid off from her factory employment. She expressed much reluctance about "signing up" for unemployment benefits. To do so undermined her sense of self-reliance and self-respect. This feeling of making it on one's own easily leads to a judgmental attitude toward others who may be unable to work (in spite of their wish to do so) because they are victims of circumstances beyond their control. The claim to self-sufficiency may isolate us from the plight and the need of others and may engender within us a false sense of security which runs counter to a Christian understanding of human finitude and community.

One characteristic often attributed to the Germans and certainly displayed by the Pennsylvania Dutch is orderliness and its concomitant quality, cleanliness. St. Paul's injunction to the Corinthians is a golden text for the Pennsylvania Dutch: "Let all things be done decently and in order" (1 Cor. 14:40). A second text, which is not biblical but which is equally pertinent, is: "Cleanliness is next to godliness." I would often hear this or that person described as being "very particular." That meant that he or she possessed the virtues of orderliness and cleanliness in abundant measure. The semi-annual housecleaning ritual which most women did "with a vengeance" was further evidence of the high position given to these traits. Many times I heard it said about a woman that she was a "good housekeeper," which implied that her house was always clean and in order. Harsh judgments were often expressed about those who did not measure up to these high standards, and there was subtle and not so subtle social pressure against those who did not "conform." Having grown up in this milieu, I confess that this orientation is very much a part of me. To be sure, these practices carried to extreme can reflect certain psychological aberrations. Just as there are alcoholics and workaholics, so there are "orderaholics" and "cleanaholics," to coin some terms. A preoccupation with order and cleanliness may be symptomatic of deep-seated psychological needs. And of course, the opposite traits of disorderliness and slovenliness are in the same category.

The Pennsylvania Dutch are perhaps best known for their food and their cooking. Even a casual tourist or observer soon bcomes aware that these people "live well." And one of the highest marks of living well is eating well. If one needs evidence of this fact, a visit to any one of the numerous farmers' markets in the Pennsylvania Dutch country will be convincing beyond doubt. Or better still, eat at one of the many establishments which feature "Pennsylvania Dutch cooking." Among these are Zinns Diner, the Akron Restaurant, Good and Plenty, Plain and Fancy, and Willow Valley, to mention only a few. Pennsylvania Dutch food is not exotic, but it is always "good and plenty." Meat, potatoes, and gravy are basic. Add to these choice vegetables and rich desserts. As I remember it, the Pennsylvania Dutch never ate many salads, but desserts were another matter. To conclude a Pennsylvania Dutch meal with just one dessert is well-nigh "heretical." Rather, there is usually an abundance of pies, cakes, and puddings. While many Pennsylvania Dutch stress such virtures as thrift, the simple life, and temperance, food and eating have always been notably excepted from these restraints.

Among the most popular and widely-participated-in forms of recreation in our country are hunting and fishing. My father engaged in both with considerable vigor, and while I never became much of a fisherman, some of my most cherished memories are of days afield with my father. Locally, father fished for bass and other fish in the Cocalico, Conestoga, and

Middle Creeks. Occasionally he and others would go to the larger Susquehanna River. For a number of years, he and several other Akronites had Maryland fishing licenses. Most of the fishing in Maryland was done at Conowingo Dam where striped bass or rockfish was the most sought-after species. Once my father caught an 18½-pound rockfish. The story of that catch was told many times. He mounted the head and it served as a reminder of that eventful day. The fishing trips to Conowingo were usually on the weekends and I accompanied the fishermen frequently.

But it was hunting that captured my interest more than fishing. My father kept beagles and became something of an authority on their breeding and training. Unlike today, pheasants were abundant in Lancaster County. It was not unusual to drive around early in the morning before the hunting season and see 100 to 200 cock pheasants. Roast pheasant is a delicacy, and our family usually had its good share. Rabbits were never as plentiful in Lancaster County as they were in other counties to the west and north. Our favorite place for rabbit hunting was Adams County, and some of my most pleasurable and unforgettable experiences were in connection with these hunts.

With more intensive farming and the conversion of more and more habitat into housing, highways, and shopping centers, hunting is not what it once was, and future prospects are uncertain. It is somewhat disconcerting to return to old haunts, filled with pleasant memories, only to find them "developed" or in the process of being "developed." Then, too, hunting has become a more controversial issue. There are many, and their numbers are probably increasing, who feel strongly that killing game animals is a violation of nature and is contrary to a sound philosophy of conservation. On the other side are those who contend that hunting is a planned and responsible method of conserving game and is less ruthless than nature's "survival of the fittest."

For the plain people and those who manifest a reverence for life, hunting is an ambiguous practice, fraught with both positive and negative implications. This tension is never easily resolved.

For the native Americans and the early European settlers, hunting was a major means of securing food. For them it was a necessity; for us, it is not. We have made it a sport, a recreation; and the food we derive from hunting is quite incidental.

Indeed, the price per pound of game meat is phenomenal when one considers the cost of licenses, clothing, guns, ammunition, and travel. It would be far more economical to buy one's meat at the grocery store than to hunt for it.

To kill a beautiful animal such as a pheasant, a grouse, or a deer is to violate God's creation. There is a sense of sadness and even guilt that attends the killing of an animal which one moment was vibrant and alive and the next is limp and lifeless. But the same is true of the slaughter of cattle, hogs, and fowl. Thus, if I want to be consistent, I must be a vegetarian and refrain from eating meat.

We tend to idealize and romanticize nature and forget that nature can be a ruthless taskmaster. If animals are not harvested by hunting, nature will do its own harvesting. Nature maintains a balance between the numbers of a given species and their habitat. If, for example, an animal population is too large for its habitat to carry, nature will weed out the excess through predation and starvation. In the realm of nature, the prevailing law is the survival of the fittest.

Many who reject the notion of a special revelation through sacred writings or the incarnation of God in a historical person, nevertheless find in nature a beauty, an orderliness, and a harmony, in which they discern the power and presence of the divine. The divine is seen and experienced in the beauty of a sunset, in a peaceful lake at dawn, in the hills ablaze with autumn's colors, and in a graceful deer or a brightly-hued bird. But this is only one side of nature. The other side is marked by violence, destruction, and death. If nature's beauty reveals the divine, what about the predation of one species upon another, the earthquakes, hurricanes and tornadoes, floods, and erupting volcanoes? These, too, are very much a part of nature. Just as there is beauty and harmony, so also there is ugliness and disharmony in nature. Nature both creates and destroys, and the orderly harvest of game animals through hunting may be more humane than nature's uncertain course.

There is another dimension to hunting which those who have never hunted cannot appreciate. To hunt is not to be a spectator, but a participant. To match one's skills and senses with those of the quarry hunted can be a creative and fulfilling experience. And more often than not, the hunted succeeds in outwitting the hunter. It is not so much the kill but the hunt that is rewarding. To be together with others out in nature and to participate in a common venture, these are the memories that outlast the statistics of game taken. At least it is so for me. To hunt with others is to know them in a new way, and it is to participate in and experience comradeship and community.

Even though I enjoy hunting, I have never been able to identify with those who resist any effort to register guns by making an appeal to their "constitutional right to keep and bear arms." Given the violence and our appalling homicide rate in comparison with other countries, I think that the registration of guns is wholly justified. While it is true that criminals will still get guns, I have little doubt that gun registration nationwide would serve to reduce the violence and the killings. If I am willing to register my automobile, which may be a more lethal weapon than a gun, why is it so unthinkable that I should also register my guns? The notion that I need a revolver under my pillow or beside my bed in order to deter intruders is an illusion. I know of no more certain way of being injured or killed than to confront an intruder with a gun. The nonviolent and nonresistant tradition of the plain people offers a more viable alternative. When confronted with a "violent" person, moral suasion, nonresistance, and accepting violation of one's property are more effective "strategies" then meeting violence with violence. Such a response is also in keeping with the teaching and the lifestyle of Jesus.

When a minister moves into a community, he or she is usually given much help and useful information by the parishioners. One ministerial acquaintance of mine moved into a pastorate in one of the nation's capital's "desirable" suburbs, whereupon one of his parishioners advised him to get a gun because "this is a dangerous neighborhood." That is not the sort of advice that gladdens the heart of any minister committed to the ministry of reconciliation!

Pennsylvania is the nation's leading deer hunting state, and every year hundreds of thousands of residents and nonresidents take to the woods and fields in search of the game. The first day of the deer season is something of an institution. Public schools in the central and northern counties of the state are closed. There is a mass migration from the more urbanized areas to the "deer mountains" where many hunters have camps. Others stay at motels or private homes. Some leave early in the morning and drive to their hunting site and return home the same day. Others spend a week in camp.

At any rate, the night before the season opens is usually the most sleepless of the year, what with visions of bucks with trophy racks and the eagerness and excitement which accompanies every opening day. However, the motivation of those who go to camp is by no means uniform. Some are zealously committed to the hunt and go exclusively for that purpose. For others, deer camp affords an opportunity to be "with the boys" and away from wives and children. Here one can talk about and listen to reports of other years, of big bucks that were gotten, or as is often the case, of those that got away. But to go to one's deer stand on a cold winter's morning and there await the dawn and the hopeful sighting of deer, is an experience quite unlike any other. It is one not soon forgotten and one worthy of passing on to future generations.

During my childhood and youth, Akron was surrounded by farms and small woods and within a few minutes one could be hunting in prime rabbit and pheasant habitat. But following World War II there was a change as more and more of the adjoining area was "developed." A local merchant was mostly responsible for Akron's growth during this period. He had extensive land holdings south of town and "developed" this area. This impetus grew and one by one the surrounding farms were subdivided and new construction resulted. The little town on the hill, which had about 700 inhabitants in the 1930s, has become a rapidly growing heterogeneous community with a population today of about 3,500. The woods through which we used to walk and play are now largely gone. Houses have been built in them and in the largest of the woods is a large hotel. One of Akron's most notable additions is a memorial park named for one who was the school principal for many years. While Akron has grown and prospered economically, it has never had a library and this represents a cultural and intellectual lag.

As noted earlier, the churches in Akron were of Germanic origin. There was little ecumenical activity with the exception of the annual Holy Week services. From Monday through Friday of Holy Week there were community services held in a different church each evening with the preacher being from another church than the one hosting the service. On Easter morning, there was a community sunrise service held at the Evangelical Church. These services began during the 1930s and continue to the present. It appears that attendance has fallen off in more recent years. I remember that there were a number of persons who had "perfect attendance" at the Holy Week services and each year on the last evening they were given special recognition.

Our family were members of the Church of the Brethren or, as it was often called by outsiders, the Dunkard Church. The term "Dunkard" derived from the Brethren practice of baptizing by "dunking" or immersion. My grandmother who lived with us from the time I was a child was a member of the Church of the Brethren. She dressed in the traditional Brethren garb, wearing a prayer veil with strings tied under the chin and a long dress with cape and apron. My mother, who attended worship and Sunday school with some regularity, was not a member until she and I were baptized when I was 18 years of age. My father came from Berks County and was of Lutheran background, although he was not an active church-man until he joined the Akron Church of the Brethren when I was 21 years of age. He had a dramatic conversion experience which was precipitated by my leaving home to enter Civilian Public Service during World War II. Being an only child, my leaving was a traumatic experience for my parents. Just at the time I left, a revival meeting was in progress at the Akron Church of the Brethren and my father "went forward" during this meeting. This was a "high moment" in both my father's and the church's experience. It was William James who spoke of "once-born" and "twice-born" persons. The person who is "once-born" grows into the Christian faith through the nurture of family and church and becomes a Christian without ever being otherwise. But the "twice-born" are those like the Apostle Paul who experience a radical change and reversal in their life so that they are converted or born again. My father's experience was of the latter type.

Except for the Lutheran Church, each of the Akron churches conducted revival meetings. The Church of the Brethren had a two-week meeting each spring and fall. In an earlier time, these meetings had almost as much of a social function as a religious one. Visiting ministers from surrounding Brethren congregations would attend and as many as possible were invited to participate in the service. In addition, lay persons from other Brethren congregations as well as persons from other local churches of various denominations were in attendance. There were usually a few "sinners" in the congregation, and they of course were potential converts. These were the days before the Brethren became as acculturated as they are now. Consequently, large numbers of young people attended these meetings, particularly on Saturday and Sunday evenings. It was at these gatherings that many a young person found a life companion.

Some meetings were better attended than others. This was due to several factors. Some evangelists were more popular than others and had a wider appeal. Sometimes there were more "decisions for Christ" than at other times, and this built up interest and attendance. Among my most graphic reminiscences are some of these revival meetings during which interest and attendance would build up until the final weekend when people would come from far and near—particularly young people. Sometimes there was standing room only, and at the conclusion of such a meeting almost everyone would attest that they had been part of a spiritual and social happening. This was a vital part of the spiritual milieu of my childhood and youth.

Today, the situation is different. No longer do the young people "swarm" to the revival meetings as they once did. Other institutions such as movies, concerts, parties, dances, and television now have priority. Moreover, the meetings are now primarily attended by the "saved," and the "sinners" attend only infrequently. This means that revivals are not the effective evangelistic technique that they once were. Consequently, new forms of evangelism and styles of witnessing must be explored and practiced if persons are to be "won to Christ."

As revival meetings go, the Brethren ones were generally "very orderly." That is, there was little show of outward emotion with the attendant "amens," "hallelujahs," and "praise the Lords." Occasionally there were tears and even sobs when someone "accepted Christ," but by and large "things were done decently and in order."

With the Evangelicals and the Zion Children's Church the situation was otherwise. Traditionally, these groups expressed more emotion in their worship, and this was particularly true at revival time. Compared with earlier practices, by my time the Evangelicals had already become more sedate. However, I remember hearing accounts about certain Evangelicals who would become "happy" especially during revival meetings or during the annual Watch Night services which observed the passing of an old year and the coming of a new one.

It was the Zion Children's revivals which were the most spirited. In addition to the faithful who were always present, there were also usually a number of curious onlookers. They would come to observe what they considered to be the curious antics of the faithful. It happened occasionally that one of them came "under conviction" and was transformed from bystander to participant.

One basic difference between the Church of the Brethren and the Evangelical and Zion Children's revivals was that in the latter one had to go forward to the altar and "pray through" in order to be "saved." To "pray through" meant that you prayed until you felt released from sin and guilt. The Brethren practice was merely to stand or to go forward and shake the evangelist's hand during the "invitation hymn."

As I look back upon those days from a longer and perhaps broader perspective, I realize that Akron's religious orientation was largely individualistic and pietistic. The emphasis was upon "getting saved" and upon a "practical Christianity," stressing such virtues as temperance, honesty, integrity, thrift, and diligence. The Lutherans, with their liturgy and the traditional Lutheran insistence upon the supremacy of faith rather than works, provided a slightly different accent. The Brethren reflected a sensitivity about peace and about the relief of human suffering, which added another dimension. Each of the churches were cognizant of "foreign missions" as this was still the heyday of the missionary movement. Almost totally absent, however, was the church's concern about such issues as racial and economic injustice and the church's involvement in the conflict between labor and management. About the only "political" issue that stirred the churches was voting on local option. Little if anything was preached or said in the churches when certain workers at the local industry were fired or threatened with dismissal because they struck for higher wages. The imbalance of emphasis between private virtues and social justice was not unique to Akron. It persists in the wider church to this present time.

The congregation which I knew best was the Akron Church of the Brethren. I was nurtured in the Sunday school and participated in the worship and other activities. It was in the context of this community that during a revival meeting I was "born again" at 18 years of age. I still recall vividly the exhilaration of that moment when I "stood" during the singing of the "invitation hymn." It gave one the unique feeling of being "clean" and of facing the future with a new and fresh perspective. The essence of the revival experience is expressed by Paul: "The old has passed away; behold the new has come" (1 Cor.

5:17). But one can't live for a lifetime in the glow of one ecstatic experience. Rebirth and renewal must occur not once, but again and again.

The Akron Church membership was composed largely of farmers, factory workers, and housewives. It was served by a so-called "free ministry." The ministers were called from the congregation and performed their ministerial functions in addition to their regular vocations. There were usually three or four ministers and they took turns preaching so that each preached about once a month.

Among my most meaningful experiences were the semi-annual love feasts. The Church of the Brethren observes a unique threefold service and attempts to reenact the events which transpired in the Upper Room on the last night of Jesus' life. The love feast service begins with feetwashing, which is followed by a fellowship meal, and concludes with communion.

At Akron the love feast was held in the sanctuary of the church. The pews were so constructed that the backs could be turned so that tables were formed. The sexes were separated, with men and boys on one side and women and girls on the other. Only baptized members participated. Those who wished to observe were welcome to do so, and they sat in Sunday school rooms in the rear. It was not unusual to have observers from the community who were not members of the Church of the Brethren. It was a "closed communion," so that only members in "good standing" in the Church of the Brethren could participate.

The love feast was a two-day service which began on Saturday afternoon and concluded with the Sunday morning worship service. Several visiting ministers were given a special invitation to attend. In addition, it was not uncommon for a number of other ministers to be in attendance. The love feast began on Saturday afternoon with a service of "self-examination." The 11th chapter of 1 Corinthians was the basis for this service and especially the injunction, "Let a man examine himself and so eat of the bread and drink of the cup." One of the visiting elders preached a "self-examination sermon" in which he admonished the congregation to take a self-inventory, to repent of sins, and to become reconciled with anyone where estrangement existed. This was to be done lest one should "eat in an unworthy manner and thus profane the body and blood of Christ." Following this service there was an intermission of several hours before the love feast which was held on Saturday evening. I remember how the elder of the Akron Church would remind the faithful that during this intermission they were on "holy ground." By evening the love feast preparation was complete. For hours prior to the actual event, the sisters prepared the love feast meal. This consisted of mutton and rice soup in which there were pieces of bread. Some of the soup was set aside for the children and others who would not be participating in the love feast.

The phenomenon of memory and our ability to recall are dependent on diverse and often inexplicable factors. Among these is our sense of smell. Certain odors which emanated from the church kitchen during love feast afternoon and the time of gathering in the evening is a memory which remains with me for a lifetime. I can almost smell it now, and it brings to remembrance high spiritual experiences and fellowship with those of "like precious faith," many of whom are no longer with us.

The love feast was held in the church sanctuary. The method of bringing the food from the kitchen, which was in the basement, to the sanctuary always intrigued me. The men formed a line from the basement to the upper room and passed the soup, which was in large bowls, from one person to another. After the tables were set, the members took their places at the tables with the men on one side and the women on the other. The ministers occupied the front tables on the men's side.

The service began with the feetwashing, for which the scriptural basis was found in John 13. The feetwashing moved from one person to the next in each row. Each person's feet were washed and he or she in turn washed another's feet. The person who washed the feet of another was "girded with a towel." Following the washing there was the greeting with the "holy kiss" and usually an audible "God bless you." The feetwashing was an attempt to reenact the scene in the Upper Room and to follow literally Jesus' injunction in John 13: "If I then your Lord and Master have washed your feet, you also ought to wash one another's feet. For I have given you an example that you should do as I have done to you." It was also a dramatic symbol which pointed to purification and the virtues of humility and of serving rather than of being served.

Following the feetwashing was the fellowship meal, the *agape* or love feast. This was a reenactment of the last supper which Jesus ate with his disciples in the Upper Room and underscored the virtues of love and fellowship within the Christian community. The large bowls of soup were placed on the tables so that four people ate from the same bowl. In addition, there was mutton and bread and butter. It was somewhat incongruous that the love feast was eaten in silence and the conversation which usually attends eating together was absent. I suppose the reason for this was that, since this was a "holy" occasion, it was believed that the usual table talk would be too mundane and thus "unholy." Meditation upon the significance of the occasion and upon its theological and christological implications was more "uplifting" than conversation.

But as I look back now, I think that some significant dimensions of love and fellowship may have been neglected by eating in silence. The division between "holy" prayer and meditation and mundane or "unholy" conversation cannot easily be made. The sacred and the profane interpenetrate. Just as the material becomes sacramental and transparent to the divine, so that which appears profane and secular can become a bearer of the holy, the mysterious, and the transcendent. We come to know each other not only through worshipping together and through our "God talk," but also through the seemingly trite and "unholy" conversation of everyday. The dichotomy between sacred and secular, between redemption and creation, represents a distortion of the best insights of Christian theology.

The third part of the service was the communion. The elder who preached the self-examination sermon officiated at the communion. He was assisted by another elder who helped to distribute the bread. The bread was unleavened and was cut in long narrow strips. These strips were passed from one communicant to another, each person breaking off a piece and giving it to his or her neighbor. A common cup containing grape juice was likewise passed from one person to another. Following the communion and the singing of a hymn the service concluded and the congregation went to their homes until assembling again on Sunday morning.

The Sunday school hour preceeded the morning worship, and one of the visiting ministers usually taught the combined adult and youth classes. There followed a service of worship with one of the visiting Brethren preaching. Thus the love feast concluded—a high moment of spiritual experience for everyone, and for some, possibly the last such occasion. A poignant remembrance and experience for me was the last love feast that my father was to attend. We sat beside each other at the table; he washed my feet; we ate from the same bowl and broke bread and drank from the cup. I did not know it then, but that was the last love feast that he and I would share. Through the vision of faith and hope, that experience points beyond itself to that day when Christ shall eat anew with us and serve us in the Kingdom of God.

With the coming of World War II, many young men were confronted with the decision as to whether they would conscientiously participate or conscientiously object. These decisions precipitated upheavals in the family, the community, and the church. Having been brought up and nurtured in the Church of the Brethren, which is one of the historic peace churches, I chose the conscientious objector position. Two others from the Akron Church of the Brethren chose the same course, while others went into the armed forces. My first assignment was forestry work in the Allegheny National Forest in Pennsylvania. After five months there I transferred to a dairy farm in Montgomery County, Maryland, where I worked for almost three years. This was my first farming experience and one for which I shall always be grateful. Before being discharged in May 1946, I worked for four months as an attendant at the Veterans' Administration Hospital at Lyons, New Jersey.

My experiences in the Civilian Public Service program proved to be broadening and educational. I became exposed to persons from differing backgrounds than my own as well as to ideas and opinions which pushed back my horizons and challenged the provincialism I had accepted too complacently.

Wartime is invariably marked by intense passion and patriotic fervor. The vast majority look with suspicion and outright hostility at conscientious objectors. I recall how some acquaintances would ignore me or fail to speak when I would see them during a leave at home. On one occasion, my father, who was a veteran of World War I and who saw action in France, expressed disapproval of the stand I had taken. But while he may have disagreed with me on this issue, he and my mother accepted me and loved me. Their support, together with that of most members of the Akron Church, was a source of strength and courage during a most difficult period.

After being discharged from CPS, I worked in a shoe factory during the summer of 1946. In September, I enrolled in Elizabethtown College from which I graduated four years later. By this time my vocational interest had become quite certain. During my CPS experience I felt increasingly "called" to be a minister. This "call" came most clearly during my time on the dairy farm and was confirmed by a congregational vote of the Akron Church in the fall of 1946. The customary practice of calling ministers was to take the vote of the church membership. Two visiting elders were present for a special council meeting. Each member of the church appeared before the elders and expressed his or her choice for minister. It was through this process that I was chosen and licensed to the Christian ministry.

Without doubt, the institution for which Akron is best known today and which gives to it a worldwide dimension is the Mennonite Central Committee (MCC). MCC was founded in 1920 and has had its headquarters in Akron since 1935. It is the cooperative relief and service agency of 17 North American Mennonite and Brethren in Christ churches. MCC coordinates and administers programs in overseas relief, education, medicine, peace, agriculture, and community development. Domestic programs supply volunteers for social and educational services in the inner-city, family and medical services in Appalachia, and for institutions working with the emotionally disturbed and retarded. It coordinates a disaster service and mental health program, and promotes the peace testimony on such matters as war, race relations, and industrial conflicts.

MCC has over 700 personnel serving one- to three-year assignments in about 40 countries. In North America, volunteers are involved in economic development education and social service programs in cities such as Toronto and Atlanta and in rural areas like Appalachia and Newfoundland. Volunteers outside North American are concentrated in Third World countries. Teachers, engineers, nurses, agriculturalists, social workers, and other persons with special training stimulate long-term change, promoting a better life for local families, communities, and churches.

Agricultural development and water conservation projects are a response to the ever-increasing need for food in Asia, Africa, and Latin America. Communities receive health and family planning education through programs in these continents. Volunteers help staff schools in Jamaica, Bolivia, the Middle East and a number of African countries, and work at development and service in conflict areas such as the Middle East.

Material aid is also provided for the immediate needs of people throughout the world. Mennonite farmers contribute wheat, beans, and meat to be canned in MCC's portable canner. Victims of recent and continuing conflict as well as victims of natural disasters receive priority.

Mennonite Disaster Service responds with short-term volunteers and material aid to the clean-up and housing needs which follow domestic hurricanes, earthquakes, tornadoes, and floods.

The Self-Help Program encourages local craftspeople in about 20 countries to earn their own living by producing craft items which are imported and sold in Self-Help shops across the United States and Canada.

The Exchange Visitor Program brings international young people to North America for a year to promote better international understanding through life and work here. The Sponsorship Program supports schoolchildren, their families and their communities at various locations around the world.

The Peace Section, with Canadian, United States, and international divisions, seeks to articulate the historic Mennonite and Brethren in Christ biblical peace position and apply it to issues such as militarism and the arms race, church-state relations, offender ministries, native concerns, community conflict intervention, justice and human rights. Offices in Ottawa, Ontario, and Washington, D. C., help keep Mennonites informed about national and international developments and help Mennonite groups express their views to the respective governments.

Mennonite Mental Health Services, a program which grew out of MCC's assigning conscientious objectors to mental hospital programs during World War II, coordinates and advises seven psychiatric centers and provides resources for the mentally handicapped and offenders.

All the above programs are administered through the MCC offices in Akron. They reflect creative and dynamic attempts to practice a deeply-held Anabaptist conviction that service to one's fellow humans is an integral part of Christ's teachings and of the Christian faith. These activities further testify to the persistent and on-going attempts of the Mennonites, together with the Friends and the Brethren who have similiar programs, to find peaceful and constructive alternatives to war, violence, and destruction. For these attempts and these contributions the world-wide church of Christ is indebted and grateful to the historic peace churches. Their witness is as salt and light and leaven and serves to judge us in our indifference and our insensitivity, and to inspire us to a more vital discipleship.

Returning to Akron, as I occasionally do, I find it almost a "strange land." It is so different from the small, heterogeneous community I knew so intimately during my childhood and youth. The fact of growth strikes me most forcefully. It is no longer the little town on the hill, but it has expanded so that all the areas around the hill are now filled with new houses. The view from the hill across the surrounding countryside is also different. Whereas it was once dotted with barns and farmhouses with wide spaces between, now it is congested with new housing, shopping centers, and business establishments of every description.

In the closing verses of 1 Corinthians 13 Paul reflected upon the imperfect and the perfect, upon the finite and the infinite, and upon time and eternity. He characterized human finitude as being marked by partial and imperfect knowledge and as seeing in a mirror dimly. But contrasted to the imperfect and the finite, Paul envisioned a time when the imperfect will pass away and when we shall see clearly and understand fully. In Hebrews 11, Abraham's pilgrimage is described in a similar way. He left his homeland not knowing where he was to go. He sojourned in a foreign land and lived in tents. But by faith he moved toward the land of promise, for he "looked forward to the city which has foundations, whose builder and maker is God." Our finitude reflects both misery and grandeur. To experience the imperfect is to catch a vision of the perfect. To know partially and to see dimly is to hope for perfection of knowledge and clarity of vision. The human pilgrimage is marked by the tension between what is and what ought to be, between what we are and what we can become. We are always on the way and the goal is ever before us. Paul said that he pressed on toward the goal for the prize of the upward call of God in Christ Jesus. To be human is to experience finitude and limitation, but it is also to search for "salvation," to move toward wholeness and a fuller realization of our essential humanity. It is these dichotomies which reflect the mysterious depths and heights of human misery and grandeur.

For me, as much as any other experience, that of returning to one's former home embodies these realities. Thomas Wolfe observed that "you can't go home again." Try as we may, that is the case. The rapidity of change sweeps away the familiar landmarks. One grows older so quickly, and the friends and acquaintances of seemingly only yesterday are too soon gone. "Time like an everflowing stream bears all its sons and daughters away." Returning home confronts us starkly with the contrast between what is and what was. The small, homogeneous town on the hill of yesterday has become the widespread heterogeneous community of today. The relatively open countryside of former years is now filled with housing and commercial development. The pace has quickened, the community has grown, values have changed, and one is confronted with the jarring realization that no, you can never go home again. There is pathos in this and a gnawing sense of insecurity and homesickness. For after all, we are finite. We cannot shape destiny. We are swept along by forces that are beyond our control. But finitude can be the doorway that leads to grace. "We are not our own, but we have been bought with a price." Our being and our destiny reside ultimately in the power and wisdom of Another whose will and whose ways are so many times not ours. To confront our finitude with the faith and the trust that we do not walk this lonesome valley alone and that there is a grace greater than all our sinful blundering, is the gateway to salvation. Our experiences of estrangement and pangs of homesickness point toward a "Kingdom" and an order of existence where the imperfect shall give way to the perfect and where we shall "understand fully even as we have been fully understood."

Amid the varied changes which have encroached upon the Plain People and the Pennsylvania Dutch of Lancaster County, there is one institution which has persisted. That is, "the *buggies* still run." Buggies represent a twofold purpose. Obviously, they are a means of transportation. But they also symbolize a tradition and a cluster of beliefs and values. They are a visible protest against the onrush of modernity and "progress." Buggies are the most visible and dramatic representation of a rigorous sectarianism which focuses on Jesus and his style of life as the "new law."

One might interpret buggies in sacramental terms. St. Augustine offered the well-known designation of a sacrament as a visible form of inward grace. Sacraments are visible elements which point to and participate in spiritual realities. We are beings who are more at home with the symbolic than the rational. Reality becomes "real" for us through signs, pictures, and symbols. H. Richard Niebuhr pointed out that man as language-user, thinker, interpreter of nature, artist, worshipper, seems to be always symbolic man, metaphor-using, image making, and image-using man.

While the Plain People traditionally have rejected symbolism and sacramentalism, nevertheless, their buggies can be regarded sacramentally. *They* are visible signs of invisible grace. Beyond their utilitarian role, they point to such inward graces as simplicity and nonconformity. They are more in harmony and at peace with the natural world than is our burgeoning technology which exploits and despoils nature.

For most of the tourists who flock to Lancaster County, the buggies of the Plain People are a curious and quaint oddity in the midst of an advanced and sophisticated society. For many of the country's residents the buggies are regarded as a traffic hazard and an obstruction to fast and efficient travel. One recent observer referred to the Amish tradition as a "fossilized tradition."

Maybe, however, we should take a second look at the buggies and the tradition and values they symbolize. Our society has long since gone beyond the "horse and buggy age," and there is no return to the agrarian economy of yesterday. But the buggies can still serve as reminders of our spiritual poverty in the midst of our vaunted scientism and materialism.

In a time of blatant waste of our natural resources and their potential scarcity and depletion, the buggies can remind us of the virtues of simplicity, of conservation, of the harmonious relationship between humans and nature.

In a time of "wars and rumors of war," of violence, and the real possibility of our annihilation at the press of a button, the buggies can remind us that peace is now our only alternative. The buggies also represent a tradition which says to us that the way of Jesus and the coming Kingdom are characterized by "peace on earth, goodwill to men" (Luke 2:14). The buggies hopefully point to that day when "nation shall not lift up sword against nation, neither shall they learn war anymore" (Isa. 2:4; Micah 4:3).

In a time marked by alienation, estrangement, loneliness, and dehumanization, the buggies point to a people who embody strong and vibrant communal and familial roots and solidarity. Their *Gemeinde* is known for its integrity, caring, and love — qualities which the world can neither give nor take away.

It is customary to dismiss the buggies as a quaint carryover from an age that we romanticize and to which at times we regress. But might it be that the buggies can be "sacramental" —visible signs of inward grace? For they can remind us again that the Kingdom of God is marked by simplicity of devotion and commitment, by peace and righteousness, by love and service. If this is so, then we rejoice and are thankful that *the buggies still run*.